THE JOKER IS WILDE!
AND HE'S NEVER BEEN SO RACY, SO
RIOTOUS, SO LAUGH-OUT-LOUD
FUNNY!
LET THE GOOD TIMES ROLL!
CLOSE THE DOOR AND GET READY
FOR FUN! THE JOKES ARE HOT,
THE GAGS ARE GROSS AND THE
LAUGHS ARE LEWD,
IN LARRY WILDE'S WILDEST
COLLECTION YET!

OFFICIAL BOOK OF
JOHN JOKES

OFFICIAL BOOK OF JOHN JOKES

Larry Wilde

Illustrations by Ron Wing

BANTAM BOOKS

TORONTO · NEW YORK · LONDON · SYDNEY · AUCKLAND

OFFICIAL BOOK OF JOHN JOKES

A Bantam Book / February 1985

ISBN 0-553-24712-3

Published simultaneously in the United States and Canada

Bantam Books are published by Bantam Books, Inc. Its
trademark, consisting of the words "Bantam Books" and the
portrayal of a rooster, is Registered in U.S. Patent and Trade-
mark Office and in other countries. Marca Registrada. Ban-
tam Books, Inc., 666 Fifth Avenue, New York, New York
10103.

PRINTED IN THE UNITED STATES OF AMERICA

O   0 9 8 7 6 5 4 3 2 1

For Ziccardi, Cornetta and
Rutledge—the three nicest
Johns around.

CONTENTS

While you're sitting here, this is your chance to read about what's going on in the crazy world out there:

Nymphomania

What's the difference between a good girl and a nice girl?

A good girl goes home and goes to bed, and a nice girl goes to bed and goes home.

*   *   *

Did you hear about the Vegas showgirl who says she has sex insomnia? She just can't keep her thighs closed.

*   *   *

Dolores and Erica were having lunch in the company cafeteria. "I had bad vibes last night," said Dolores.

"Boyfriend worries?" asked Erica.

"No, my intimate massager short-circuited."

*   *   *

SEX

The poor man's polo

*   *   *

Sharon, a shapely steno in Seattle, saved her money for years in order to have a two-week vacation in glorious Hawaii.

When she returned to Seattle and hurried off the plane, she was greeted by Andrea, her closest friend. The two girls flew into a wild embrace and Andrea blurted, "Quick, tell me! What was the most exciting thing that happened to you in the whole trip?"

"Let me think a sec! Oh, I know! I was gang-banged in a pup tent!"

"Reeeeeeeally!" cried the friend. "What's a pup tent?"

*   *   *

Did you hear about the girl who sat on Pinnochio's face and said, "Lie to me"?

*   *   *

What is the difference between *kinky* and *perverted?*

Kinky—you use a feather.

Perverted—you use the whole chicken.

*   *   *

A beach boy who loved to have fun
Kept screwing a girl in the sun.
    While his ass, being bare,
    Cooked to medium rare,
The girl kept exclaiming, "Well Done!"

*   *   *

Loretta had buried three husbands, so when she reached 40 she decided to give up her surburban lifestyle and join the Hells Angels.

At the motorcycle hideout, the boss Angel, Big Mike, asked her, "Can you ride a bike?"

Without answering, Loretta hopped on a motorcycle and performed some of the fanciest bike riding the gang had ever witnessed.

"Okay," said Big Mike, "can you fight?"

"Bring on your best!" answered Loretta.

She then proceeded to beat up three six-foot bruisers by laying each one out with karate chops.

"Not bad," admitted Big Mike. "Have you ever been picked up by the fuzz?"

"No," said Loretta, "but I've been swung around by the tits a few times!"

*   *   *

How can you tell the difference between male chromosomes and female chromosomes?

Just pull down their genes!

*   *   *

"Gee guys," said Snow White, "I've always dreamed of getting seven inches—but not an inch at a time!"

*   *   *

What's red and has seven dents?
Snow White's cherry.

*   *   *

What do you get if you cross a rooster and a telephone pole?
A 30-foot cock that wants to reach out and touch someone.

*   *   *

A show girl with features cherubic
Was famed for her area pubic.
    When they asked her its size
    She replied in surprise,
"Are you speaking of square feet, or cubic?"

*   *   *

What do Jell-O and women have in common?

They both quiver when you eat them.

* * *

What's the speed limit on Highway 69?
Lickity-split.

* * *

Emily sat in the handsome lawyer's office explaining her case.

"I became pregnant and had to have an abortion," she admitted, "because of a defective diaphragm."

"What do you want me to do?" he asked.

"Well," she cooed, "you could start by revisiting the scene of the accident."

* * *

What was the first obscenity heard on TV?

"Ward, weren't you a little hard on the Beaver last night?"

* * *

1st coffee bean: I like to be made instant.
2nd coffee bean: Not me, I prefer the regular grind.

Bruce Merrin, Hollywood's Premier Publicist, gets guffaws with this mirthmaker:

Marlene, a magnificently stacked brassiere model, strolled into a singles' bar wearing a pair of super tight-fitting pants. You could see every pulsating part of her flesh as she slithered up to a bar stool and sat down.

Rick, sitting right beside her, said, "Wow, baby, how do you get into those pants?"

"Well," said Marlene, "you can start by buying me a vodka on the rocks."

PATIENCE IS THE DIFFERENCE BETWEEN RAPE AND SEDUCTION!

VOYEUR

*A person who thinks privacy is
a spectator sport*

* * *

Little Bobby spied two dogs locked in intercourse, and was watching them with great interest when his father came along.

"You know, son," said the embarrassed parent, "that's the real lesson of the Good Samaritan. The dog on top is sick, and the dog on the bottom is helping carry him to the hospital."

"I guess you're right, Dad," said Bobby. "But isn't it funny? Any time you try to help somebody else you always end up getting it in the ass."

* * *

What did the Kotex say to the condom?
"If you break, we both go out of business."

* * *

One night during a Boston Pops Concert, Arthur Fiedler became quite exasperated with the performance of a beautiful female cellist. Suddenly he cried out, "Young lady, there you sit with that God-given instrument between your legs and all you can do is scratch it!"

Did you ever stop to think that if the Pilgrims had shot bobcats instead of turkeys for food, we'd all be eating pussy for Thanksgiving?

* * *

"How's yore sex life?" asked a hillbilly.

"Well," said his neighbor, "I've been screwing so long with a limber dick, I swear I could row a boat with a rope."

* * *

Farmer Gibbons heard a commotion outside his living room window and peered into the twilight.

"Ida Mae!" shouted Gibbons. "That you out there in the barn?"

"Yes oof oof oof Paw oof oof oof! Hit's oof oof oof me!"

"What you doin' out there?"

"Ah'm givin' oof oof oof the hired man oof oof oof a piece OOF!"

The farmer turned to his wife. "That gol dern young'un," he said. "Next thing you know she'll be chewin' gum."

* * *

What's *indecent?*

When it's in long, and it's in hard, and it's in deep, then it's indecent.

* * *

There was a young farm girl named Zoe
Whose lover had pulled out too slow.
    So they tried it all night
    Till he got it just right . . .
Well, practice makes pregnant, you know.

*   *   *

A tall, good-looking guy got on a Los Angeles bus and sat down next to a pretty blonde. "Hi," he said, "my name is Snow."

"My name is June," replied the girl.

"Say, wouldn't it be nice to have seven inches of Snow in the middle of June?"

"Yes," answered the blonde, "but wouldn't it be slushy in the middle of June after seven inches of snow had come and gone?"

*   *   *

The waitress called out to the short-order cook, "Come again on the rice pudding!"

"You do, and I won't eat it!" shouted the customer.

*   *   *

For a rose to smell like a pussy
    Is very, very rare,
But for a pussy to smell like a rose,
    You've Got Something There!

*   *   *

What did the potato chip say to the battery?

I'm Frito Lay if you're EverReady.

*　　*　　*

Two Martians landed on the outskirts of San Diego one night. They looked around and spotted a gasoline station with a bright red gas pump out in front.

"You stay here," said one Martian. "I'll go talk to him."

He walked over and planted himself in front of the red gas pump and said, "Which way to your capital city?"

A few minutes later he rejoined his companion.

"Well, what did he say?" asked the other Martian.

"He didn't say anything. He just stood there with his prick in his ear."

*　　*　　*

March is National Cat Month.
Make somebody's pussy happy.

*　　*　　*

What's the only bad thing about oral sex?
The view.

*　　*　　*

Stanley, the New York piece-goods salesman, was having a late dinner in a Houston restaurant. Laverna, his waitress, was attractive and well built. Stanley believed in the hard sell. He was a man of action. He winked at the waitress and she smiled, and he asked her if she'd like to go for a ride after work.

She agreed, and soon they were in his car heading for the countryside. Stanley left the main road and quickly found a secluded spot. He stopped the car, turned off the motor and said, "Shall we screw?"

"Well," said the girl, "I usually don't, but you've sweet-talked me into it."

If you're speaking of actions immoral,
Then how about giving the laurel
　　To mighty Queen Esther,
　　No three men could best her—
One fore, and one aft, and one oral?

*　　*　　*

Did you hear about the blind man who walked into a fish market and exclaimed, "Hello girls."

*　　*　　*

Old Mrs. Coleman, the neighborhood busybody, stopped little Norman and asked, "What are you learning in elementary school these days, young man?"

"Since there's sex education now, too, Mrs. Coleman," answered the youngster, "we learn all about reading, writing and a rhythmic dick."

*　　*　　*

OFFICE MONKEY

A girl who holds her job by her tail

*　　*　　*

Garwood, a Madison Avenue advertising exec, was sitting at a bar when he noticed Betty on a stool near him. He started a conversation, and soon offered her $1,000 to spend the weekend with him at his home.

Betty accepted. After the weekend was over, she asked him for the money, and he said he'd mail a check for the amount.

The check arrived, but it was only for $500. Betty went straight to his office. It was full of people. Not wanting to embarrass him, she said, "In regard to that house you rented—I received only half the rent."

Garwood caught on and said, "Oh yes, the house. Well, first of all, you didn't tell me it had been used, secondly it was too big, and third, there was no heat."

"First of all," said the girl, "you didn't ask if it had been used. Second, it wasn't too big, you just didn't have enough furniture to fill it, and third there was plenty of heat, you just didn't know how to turn it on."

P.S. She got the other $500.

* * *

What is the difference between men and jelly beans?
Jelly beans come in colors.

* * *

HOT TUB

A balling bowl

* * *

15

Why can't trains have little trains like people have little people?

Because trains always pull out on time.

* * *

There was a young girl of Mobile
Whose hymen was made of chilled steel.
    To give her a thrill
    Took a rotary drill
Or a number 9 emery wheel.

* * *

What is the difference between herpes and AIDS?

Herpes is a love story. AIDS is a fairy tale.

* * *

"Did you know an elephant has sex organs in his feet?"

"Really?"

"Yeah. If he steps on you—you're screwed!"

* * *

What's the difference between love and herpes?

Herpes lasts forever.

* * *

Two canaries in a cage. "Hey," said the male, "let's screw."
"No."
"Why not?"
"I've got chirpies."

* * *

What do you get if you fuck a midget?
Twerpies.

* * *

What do you get if you fuck ice cream?
Slurpies.

* * *

What do a Seiko watch and an elephant have in common?
They both come in quartz.

* * *

What does an elephant use for a vibrator?
An epileptic.

* * *

What is the difference between mononucleosis and herpes?
You catch mono from snatching kisses. . . .

In Africa, three missionaries, Barton, Filbert and McLaughlin, were captured by a primitive tribe. The men were bound and tied to stakes. The Witch Doctor approached Barton and said, "You have choice, White Man. Either death or *Chu Gah*!"

"I don't want to die," answered Barton, "I'll take *Chu Gah*!"

The natives took the missionary, ripped off his clothes, and forced him to get on his hands and knees. Then, one by one, all of the native men sodomized Barton.

The Witch Doctor then went to Filbert. "Which you want? Death or *Chu Gah*?"

"Please don't kill me," moaned Filbert. "I'll take *Chu Gah*."

They grabbed Filbert and once again all the men in the tribe raped him.

Finally, the Witch Doctor spoke to McLaughlin. "Now your turn. You want death or *Chu Gah*?"

"You are not going to do that to me, I'd rather die. Go ahead and kill me."

"You choose death," repeated the Witch Doctor. "All right then, you die by *Chu Gah*!"

Why don't they allow Volkswagens in Africa?

Because an elephant will screw anything with a trunk in the front.

*   *   *

"Have you ever seen an eggplant?"

"Of course."

"Well, you've been a lot farther up a chicken's ass than I have."

*   *   *

Why does an elephant have four feet?
Cause six inches won't do.

*   *   *

Why don't chickens wear underwear?
Because their peckers are on their face.

*   *   *

Helen, a Polish waitress who was really built, walked into a saloon one night after work and ordered a bottle of Budweiser.

"I love Budweiser," she told the bartender.

Four longshoremen at the bar began leering at Helen, but she paid no attention to them. She continued drinking her Budweiser until she had put down six or seven bottles, and then she suddenly just keeled right over. Out cold.

The longshoremen carried her into the back room and, one by one, took a whack at her. Then they hauled her back to the bar, revived her with a cold towel, and sent her home.

The following week she returned, and after seven or eight bottles of Bud she had passed out. The same guys were there, and once again she got a quadruple banging without knowing it.

This went on once a week for several months and then all of a sudden Helen stopped coming in. Then, one night a few weeks later, the Polish girl showed up again and the bartender said, "I suppose it'll be the usual—Budweiser?"

"No," she said, "I think I'll switch to Michelob. Budweiser seems to make my pussy sore."

*   *   *

What's the difference between a porcupine and a Porsche?

On a porcupine the pricks are on the outside.

*   *   *

There was a young waitress named Rose
Who could diddle herself with her toes.
    She did it so neat
    She fell in love with her feet,
And christened them Cletis and Mose.

21

*   *   *

SEX-DRIVE

*Trying to find a motel with
a vacancy*

*   *   *

Why do they have a string on a Tampax?
So you can floss after eating.

*   *   *

How do big Smurfs get little Smurfs?
They smuck!

*   *   *

What did the hurricane say to the palm
trees?
Hold on to your nuts, boys. This is no
ordinary blow job!

*   *   *

What do you get if you cross a shell-
fish and an owl?
A mussel that stays up all night.

*   *   *

Fagomania

While shaving in the bathroom, Byron shouted, "You know, darling, I don't seem to fit in too well with the boys at the office."

There was no reply. "You know, honey, the fellows at the office seem to feel that I'm somewhat odd."

Again there was no response. "Dear, I believe that the boys at the office think I am queer."

There was still no answer and so Byron shouted, "For heaven's sake, Sebastian, are you listening?"

*   *   *

The Gay Liberation Movement has just announced a major victory over the Weather Bureau.

Next year, the second tropical storm will be named "Hurricane Bruce."

*   *   *

Leland phoned a Northern California poultry ranch just before Thanksgiving and asked, "Do you have any gobblers?"

"No, you want my brother," replied the fowl man, "he runs the fruit farm."

*   *   *

Did you hear about the I.U.D. invented by a gay gynecologist?

He calls it a fruit loop.

*   *   *

Lance and Christopher were having a brew at a Santa Monica bar. Lance offered, "I've just read an article in a medical journal saying that sleeping with women gives you lung cancer."

"I don't believe it," said Christopher. "I mean, I just don't think that's true."

"Actually you're quite right. It isn't true," retorted Lance. "But spread it around."

*   *   *

There was a young parson named Stings
Who talked about women and things.
    But his secret desire
    Was a boy in the choir,
With a bottom like jelly on springs.

*   *   *

FRUIT FLOAT

Two fags on a water bed

*   *   *

A truck smashed into the rear end of a new Chartreuse sports car in which Rory and Austin were cruising. Rory leapt out and started screaming at the driver. The driver, looking meaner than a gorilla, shouted "Kiss my hairy ass, you cocksucker!"

Rory ran back to Austin in the sports car. "I think everything's going to be all right. He wants to settle out of court!"

*   *   *

What's the difference between a California orange and a Florida orange?

You cut 'em both in half and you suck on both of them. The one that sucks back is from California.

*   *   *

Did you hear about the King, who fell in love with the Court Jester?

He was at his wit's end.

* * *

Ronald and Pierce met at a Los Angeles bar. "How's your ass?" asked Ronald.

"Oh, shut up!" answered Pierce.

"Mine, too. It must be the smog!"

* * *

There was a young fellow named Powell
Who buggered himself with a trowel.
    The triangular shape
    Was conducive to rape,
And was easily cleaned with a towel.

* * *

Hubert and Lewis had been lovers for years. They shared a beautiful apartment, four perfectly matched poodles, barrels of the finest china and silver, and years of perfect uninterrupted bliss. Then suddenly, tragedy. Lewis got hemorrhoids.

It was a very serious case. In spite of spending a small fortune on Preparation H, nothing could be done. They went to Dr. Martin, and soon learned the dreadful news. "I'll have to operate," said the proctologist.

The day of the operation, Hubert paced

up and down in the waiting room. By accident, he spotted Alex, a mutual friend—someone they knew from orgies and the nightly doubles in the park. Hubert told all, weeping uncontrollably on the shoulder of this older, somewhat jaded friend.

"But what shall I do? We've been together for years. Oh Alex, when do you think we'll be able to have sex again?"

"Is he in a private room or a ward?"

* * *

GAY DAISY CHAIN

A swish kabob

* * *

"There's a queer here who thinks he's an owl?"

"Who?"

* * *

In San Francisco, an evangelist was delivering a flaming sermon on vice that shook the rafters of the mission. "Listen to me, all you cigarette suckers, all you bottle suckers—"

Just then a high voice lisped from the back, "Don't forget us-s-s!"

* * *

The year was 1906. Cecil walked into a San Francisco saloon and sat way at the end of the bar. As the bartender approached, Cecil lisped, "S-s-s-scotch on the rocks-s-s-s!"

"Listen mister," raged the bartender, "we don't serve your kind in this place."

Cecil simply crossed his legs and glared at the bartender. At that precise moment the earthquake hit. A chandelier dropped from the ceiling. Bottles fell behind the bar. People began screaming and running out. There was complete chaos. When the earthquake stopped the bartender stood frozen in shock.

He looked across the bar and Cecil was still sitting there glaring at him. Cecil lisped, "Now are you gonna serve me that s-s-s-scotch or shall I do it again?"

*   *   *

Jasper and Augustus were to go to a Key West masquerade party and couldn't think of what to wear.

Jasper finally broke their piggy bank and took all the money to a supermarket where he bought 20 cans of condensed milk, opened them all, and then said to his roommate, "Now throw it all over me—I'm going to the ball as a wet dream!"

*   *   *

What do they call a bouncer in a gay bar?

A flame thrower.

*   *   *

Said an airy young fairy named Jess,
"The oral requires finesse,
    While in method the anal
    Is terribly banal,
And the trousers will get out of press."

*   *   *

The answer is: Cock Robin.
The question is: Batman, what is that you're putting in my mouth?

*   *   *

What do you call a milkman who wears high heels?

A Dairy Queen.

* * *

Did you hear about the two gays in Burbank who had a misunderstanding so they went outside and exchanged blows?

* * *

Father Ramirez, an uneducated priest in San Salvador, entered the Caracas hospital with a bowel tumor. As a gag, they told him he was pregnant, and after surgery he was given the baby of an unmarried girl who had died in childbirth. The doctor told the priest that his child was delivered by Caesarean section.

The priest brought up the baby as his nephew. Years later, on his deathbed, Father Ramirez called the boy to him. "There is something I must tell you," said the priest. "You've always called me 'Father,' but now that I am about to die I have to tell you the truth. I am not really your father, I am your mother."

"Then who is my father?" asked the astounded boy.

"The Archbishop of Caracas!"

* * *

Charles: You can kiss my butt.
Thomas: I'm not ready to make up yet!

* * *

"Daddy," asked the little boy, "what does drag mean?"

"It's not important," his father replied, "just unhook my bra."

* * *

All the guests at the costume party were amused as Quentin came in the door stark naked, on roller skates, with a long string tied to his dong.

"Hey, Quentin," called out a friend, "just what are you supposed to be?"

"Isn't it obvious? . . . A pull toy!"

* * *

"Did you know fags have their own Saint now?"

"Really? How's he called?"

"St. Lavender!"

* * *

TWO GAY SCOTSMEN

Ben Doon and Phil MaCrevice

* * *

What do they call a fag from Alabama?
He's a homo sex you-all.

*   *   *

Gwen and Phillip were unable to have a baby. Since Phillip was sterile, he agreed that Gwen could take a lover so that he could get her pregnant. She was introduced to Boniface, a handsome hairdresser, and in a short time Gwen became pregnant. Nine months later she gave birth to a bouncing baby boy. Phillip, never too happy about his wife's lover being gay, went to the hospital to visit his new son.

He entered the baby display area where each infant was howling and screeching. The nurse led Phillip to his new son, who was smiling and gurgling happily.

"Say," asked Phillip, "all these other babies are crying and screaming. My kid is the only one with a big smile on his face. How come?"

"Oh," explained the nurse, "we just put a pacifier up his ass."

*   *   *

Did you hear about the new card game in Greenwich Village called Pansy Poker?

Queens are wild and straights don't count.

*   *   *

Jesse James, about to rob a train, pulled out his six shooters and marched down the aisle. "All right everybody!" he shouted. "You better get ready cause I'm gonna rape all the men and rob all the women."

A man stood up and said, "Don't you have that in reverse, Jesse? Don't you mean you're gonna rape all the women and rob all the men?"

Simon sitting way in the back piped up, "You just let Je*sse* do what she want*ssss* to do."

Bevis and Ashley were roommates and having a big fight. "You can kiss my ass goodbye!" snapped Bevis.

"And you," hissed Ashley, "can bid my tush *buns voyage*!"

* * *

There was an old priest in Madrid
Who cast loving eyes on a kid.
  Said he, "Oh my joy,
  I'll bugger that boy,
You'll see if I don't"—and he did.

* * *

A kindly, older man had brought Dennis home, and they were nestled down into the sheets. Dennis smiled up at him and said, "I'm just a minor, you know, and the pastor of our country church told all us boys about terrible big-city perverts like you, out to screw every innocent kid they can get their hands on. I thank God and Reverend Trask I finally found one."

* * *

How many gays does it take to screw in a light bulb?

Four. One to screw the bulb and three to scream, "Fabuloussss!"

* * *

What does Gay stand for?
Got AIDS Yet?

*　　*　　*

What do they call two homosexuals rolling down a hill?
Rol-*AIDS*.

*　　*　　*

Did you hear about the guy who walked into a Gay bar where they were playing loud music, and wound up with hearing AIDS?

*　　*　　*

What do they call a fag who doesn't have AIDS?
A lucky cocksucker.

*　　*　　*

Felix was looking in a sex-shop window. He saw a large rubber cock that appealed to him and went inside.

When the clerk came to wait on him, Felix pointed to the big black penis in the window. "I'll take that one," he said.

"Should I wrap it or just put it in a bag?" asked the clerk.

"Neither," said Felix. "I'll just eat it right here."

Lisped a limp-wristed cowboy named Jay,
"It's a hell of a place to be gay!
　　I must, on the prairies,
　　For shortage of fairies,
With the deer and the antelope play."

＊　　＊　　＊

Paul, sitting at a bar, noticed that Gale was quite pretty and invited her to have a drink.

"Okay," she said, "but it won't do you any good."

After they finished, Paul ordered another. After the second round, they danced for a while, then Paul said, "How about going to my place for a few drinks, and then listening to some stereo?"

"Okay, but it won't do you any good," repeated the girl.

At his apartment, they drank, listened to music and suddenly Paul asked, "Mind if I kiss you?"

As expected she replied, "Okay, but it won't do you any good."

Paul grabbed her and said, "Listen, we've been together now for over three hours. You're very appealing and I would like you for my wife!"

"Oh, that's different," exclaimed Gale, "send her right up!"

＊　　＊　　＊

*   *   *

"Do you know the difference between a cocksucker and a corned beef sandwich?"

"No."

"Good. Come over tomorrow for lunch."

*   *   *

Did you hear about the two fags who raped a girl on Rodeo Drive?

One held her down while the other styled her hair.

*   *   *

GAY HOSPITAL

Cedars of Lesbian

*   *   *

Ray walked into the house and discovered his wife, Marie, waiting for him in a negligee. She served him a martini, and then sat down on the sofa.

"What would you say," began Marie, "if I told you that I was having an affair with your best friend?"

"I'd say you were a lesbian!"

*   *   *

Nelson sat at a table in a smart Los Angeles French restaurant, studying the menu. The waiter arrived and asked, "May I take your order, sir?"

"I'll begin with the *paté*," replied Nelson. "Then the consommé, the duck *l'orange* with string beans and wild rice. No dessert. I'll have black tea and would you send me the wine steward, please?"

The waiter was writing busily on his pad. When he finished he tore off a piece of paper, set it down in front of the customer and left. Nelson picked up the paper and found the waiter had written:

"Sir, your fly is open. Two ladies just to your right have been ogling you. When I return with the paté *I will stand between you and the women long enough to give you a chance to adjust your clothing.*

P.S. I love you."

* * *

What do you call two gay guys called Bob?

Oral Roberts.

* * *

What is the difference between a bull dyke and a whale?

About five pounds and a flannel shirt.

* * *

What do you call this? (*Stick out tongue*)

A lesbian with a hard-on.

* * *

Did you hear about the fag who had a hysterectomy?

He had his teeth removed.

* * *

Sylvester strolled into a singles' bar on Santa Monica Boulevard. The next day he had lunch with his co-worker, Barnabas.

"How was it?" asked Barnabas.

"Just awful!" Sylvester complained. "There were 15 guys for every man."

* * *

*   *   *

MASOCHISM

The agony of the ecstasy

*   *   *

A motorcycle cop stopped Glascox on the highway. He leered at the police officer and pursed his lips, then grinned from ear to ear.

"Wipe that smile off your face, fella!" said the policeman.

"What!" lisped Glascox, "and ruin my makeup!"

*   *   *

Why do so many homosexuals come from Arkansas and Tennessee?

If you grew up around so many ugly gals what else would you want to be?

*   *   *

How do you seat four gays on a bar stool?

Turn it over.

*   *   *

Did you hear about the gay nudist who was such a nice guy he'd give you the tan off his back?

* * *

There once was a well-groomed young nance
Who responded to every advance,
    But rather than strip,
    He let anything slip
Through a hole in the seat of his pants.

* * *

Two huge pro-football players walked into a St. Louis lounge and noticed Ambrose, sitting at the bar. "Get that fag, outa here!" said one player to the bartender.

"He's not hurting anybody," said the barkeep.

"Never mind," said the grid star, "I'll handle it."

He walked over to the homosexual and barked, "Get outa here before I mop the deck with you."

"All right, I'll go," said Ambrose, "but I bet I can beat you in a game of Bar Football."

"You couldn't beat me in anything!" screamed the ball player. "Go ahead, what's the game?"

Ambrose ordered two glasses of beer. He lifted one, drained the glass and shouted,

"Touchdown!" Then he dropped his pants, farted, and exclaimed, "Extra point!"

The ball player laughed, picked up the glass of beer, finished it in one swallow and said, "Touchdown!" Then he dropped his pants and before he could say anything, Ambrose was sticking him in the ass, shouting, "Block that kick! Block that kick!"

Ethnomania

What is the New Yorker's motto?
"Eat, drink and be merry for tomorrow you may be killed by a Puerto Rican mugger."

* * *

How can you tell if a Puerto Rican girl is a virgin?
If she has only three kids.

* * *

Sixteen-year-old Rosita was sitting on a stoop with her friend, Maria.

"I don't know why you don't believe me," said Rosita, "but I still have my cherry."

"I didn't say I don't believe you," replied Maria, "I only want to know, does it get in the way when you make it?"

* * *

A Puerto Rican walked up to a girl and said, "What do you say to a little ass?"

"Hello little ass," replied the girl.

*   *   *

Carmen and Rickey had been married only three months when she gave birth to a bouncing baby boy.

The proud grandmother was stopped on the street one day by one of her neighbors. "Hey, I see your Carmen just had a baby after only three months," smirked the neighbor.

"You surprised?" asked the new grandmother. "My Carmen is such an innocent girl, how would she know how long to carry a baby?"

*   *   *

On the subway, how can you tell a Puerto Rican girl from a Black girl?

The Puerto Rican is the one with the long hair under her armpits.

*   *   *

Why does a Puerto Rican girl wear rollers on Saturday night?

She has a hot date on Tuesday.

*   *   *

What's three miles long and has an I.Q. of 86?

A Puerto Rican Parade.

*   *   *

A Polack, a Puerto Rican and an Italian jumped out of the Empire State Building. In what order did they reach the ground?

The Italian hit first 'cause he fell like a rock.

The Polack landed second—he had to ask directions.

The Puerto Rican came last—he stopped to write "Screw You!" on the side of the building.

*   *   *

What is the Puerto Rican National Anthem?

"We'll take Manhattan, the Bronx and Staten Island too. . . ."

*   *   *

Did you hear about the Puerto Rican secretary who is getting so experienced she can type 20 mistakes a minute?

*   *   *

PUERTO RICAN PARADE

20,000 Jews standing on Fifth Avenue
watching the help march by

*   *   *

What do they call a Puerto Rican girl
who is pretty?
Italian.

*   *   *

The world still remembers the heroic
stand made by the Italians during World
War II.
British naturalists visiting Italy recently
have brought back some amazing films showing three Italian birds surrendering to a worm.

*   *   *

Why do Italian men want to grow
moustaches?
So they can look like their mothers.

*   *   *

What's the difference between Jewish
mothers and Italian mothers?
Black stockings.

*   *   *

Gondolfo, Rizzutti and Costagna were talking on the stoop. "What's your favorite food?" asked Gondolfo.

"I like the spaghetti and meat balls that my wife Rosa makes," replied Rizzutti.

"I like Veal Marsala, and Eggplant Parmigiana with some ravioli on the side," answered Costagna. "What's your favorite food, Gondolfo?"

"Well," said the third Italian, "I like a pussy."

"Pussy? Ahh, that tastes like shit!" said Costagna.

"Maybe you take too big a bite!"

* * *

Why do Black people keep chickens in their yard?
To teach kids how to walk.

* * *

MASS CONFUSION

Father's Day in a Black neighborhood

* * *

What is Fi-Fi-Fo-Fi-Fi-Fo-Fo?
Mayor Washington's phone number!

* * *

Mrs. Jackson walked into Minetti's vegetable market and asked for five pounds of onions. "I'm a sorry," said Minetti, "we all out a onions."

The next five days in a row, Mrs. Jackson asked for onions and finally Minetti got mad and asked the woman, "Do you know how to spell?"

"Damn right," said Mrs. Jackson, "Why you askin'?"

"Well," said Minetti, "if you took a R.A.Z. out of a *raspberry,* what a you have?"

"Why, *berry* of course," answered the black woman.

"Now," said the Italian, "if you take a B.L.U.E. out of *blueberry,* what a you have?"

"Berry," said Mrs. Jackson.

"All right," said Minetti, "now, if you took the F.U.C.K. out a onions, what a you got?"

"Mister," she answered, "there ain't no fuck in onions."

"Lady, that's what I been a tryin' to tell a you all a week."

* * *

What do you get if you cross a Black with a groundhog?

Six more weeks of basketball.

* * *

"How'd you make out with that white chick last night?"

"I couldn't make head nor tail out a that gal."

"Whatch you mean?"

"She slammed the door in my face. I didn't get no head. I didn't get no tail."

*   *   *

Ronald Reagan has just come up with a way to reduce the welfare rolls. He's going to expand the NBA to 1,000 teams.

*   *   *

Reverend Perkins was expounding on the evils of sin. "Sin," he thundered, "is like a big mean ol' dog. There's the big dog of pride, the big dog of envy, the big dog of gluttony, and last there's the big mean ol' dog of sex. We got to kill all them dogs before we can get to heaven. And it can be done—I know—because I have done it, brothers. Yes, I have killed the dog of envy and the dog of pride, and I have killed the dog of gluttony, and I even killed the dog of sex!"

A voice from the back row said, "Is you sure that last dog didn't die a natural death?"

*   *   *

Slappy White, the veteran comedian, kills audiences with this hunk of hilarity:

Gomez, Goldberg and Johnson were killed in a catastrophe and wound up in heaven. Each man faced the Lord. "Will there ever be a Mexican Pope? asked Gomez.

"Yes, one day there will be a Mexican Pope," replied the Lord.

Goldberg stepped up and asked, "Will there ever be a Jewish Pope?"

"Yes," answered the Lord, "one day there will be a Jewish Pope."

"Will there ever be a Black Pope?" asked Johnson.

"Yes, there will be a Black Pope," replied the Lord, "but not as long as I'm alive."

What do you have when there are 50,000 Blacks in a stadium?

Afro Turf.

*   *   *

ENDLESS LOVE

*Stevie Wonder playing
tennis with Ray Charles*

*   *   *

Claudell walked into a doctor's office and put his penis on the desk. "What's the matter with that?" asked the M.D.

"I don't know," the black man said, "Have a look at it."

So the doctor got out his pencil, tried to pick up the penis and the pencil broke. The physician finally lifted it with steel tongs, took a quick look and announced, "V.D.!"

"That's impossible, Doc. I can't have no V.D. 'cause I use precautions."

"Look," said the doctor. "I'm just about fed up with you Black folks coming in here and telling me you can't have V.D. That is V.D. Now what precautions have you been taking?"

"I been giving her a false name and address."

*   *   *

What do you get when you cross an Eskimo, a faggot and a Black?

A snow blower that doesn't work.

*　　*　　*

Sister Agnes was grabbed by a husky Black man near the convent one evening, and he banged her three times.

After it was over she rushed to the Mother Superior and told her what happened.

"All right, sister," said the head nun. "Go down to the kitchen, get a lemon out of the refrigerator, cut it in half, and suck all the juice out of it!"

"Oh," cried Sister Agnes, "will that take care of everything?"

"No," said the Mother Superior. "But it will take that silly grin off your face."

*　　*　　*

"The whole attitude toward sex has been changing in America," said Walter to his dinner companion.

"Why do you say that?" he asked.

"I talked to a priest who said he read *The Joy of Sex*. And I said to him, 'Father, I'm shocked to think you'd buy a book like that.' He said, 'I didn't buy it—my friend Rabbi Grossman gave it to me for a wedding present.' "

*　　*　　*

A priest in the lobby of a Vegas hotel called Doreen, the voluptuous cigarette girl, over and said, "Why don't you go upstairs to my room!"

"Father, that's terrible!" said the girl.

"Oh, it's all right," said the priest, "it's in the Bible!"

So she went up. The Priest got there and said, "Why don't you take off your clothes!"

"Why father, shame on you!"

"Oh, it's all right," said the priest, "my dear, it's in the Bible!"

She took off her clothes and so did the priest and after they made love, she said, "Is that in the Bible, too?"

"Of course, my dear!"

"Well, I want to see it!"

The priest went over to the desk, took out the Gideon Bible, opened to the first page and said, "See, it's written right here: 'The cigarette girl screws!' "

A lecherous priest named McHugh
Screwed an usher's wife in a pew.
   "I'll admit I'm not pious,"
   He said, "I've a bias,
I think it's diviner to screw."

*   *   *

Bridget went to the parish priest in an agitated condition.

"I want a separation from Pat," she told him, "I have reason to believe that he has been unfaithful to me."

"What makes you think that?" asked the parish priest.

"I don't think he's the father of my last child."

*   *   *

Have you heard about the expedition of Irishmen who set out to climb Mount Everest?

They ran out of scaffolding thirty feet from the top.

*   *   *

Did you hear about the time Jesus came into a Holiday Inn, handed the night clerk three nails, and asked to be put up for the night?

*   *   *

Did you hear about that Catholic all-girl jazz band that had to disband when its rhythm section got knocked up?

*   *   *

Shapiro won $200,000 in the Irish Sweepstakes. His accountant explained he'd have to pay income taxes on it, but if he moved to Ireland he would not have to pay a penny in taxes. So he moved to Ireland.

When a year passed Shapiro was able to apply for citizenship papers. He was given a physical examination and was refused citizenship because of the fact that he had been circumcised.

Shapiro addressed a letter to Ireland's government. He started by narrating what had happened, and then he wrote:

"In my country, the United States, I already know that a man has to be one hundred percent Protestant to become a Mason. He has to be a hundred percent Catholic to join the Knights of Columbus. But this is the first time I ever heard a man has to be one hundred percent prick to be an Irishman."

*   *   *

If Tarzan and Jane were Jewish what would Cheeta be?

A fur coat.

*　　*　　*

Flanagan had been drinking all night with the boys and was afraid to go home. "Don't worry, me bucko," advised a pal, "just walk in the house, grab her and make love to her. She won't say a word about your havin' a few with the boys."

Flanagan staggered home, grabbed his wife, and threw her down on the living-room sofa. Then he ripped off her clothes and kissed her on both ears. Then he kissed her neck. Then he kissed her shoulders. Then he kissed each breast. Then he kissed her belly button. Then he kissed her knee.

His wife snapped, "If that was a bar you wouldn't have passed it up!"

*　　*　　*

Father McGinty, Reverend Meese and Rabbi Gottesman were having a discussion about the meaning of life. "For us," said the priest, "life begins at conception."

"That's fair," agreed the minister, "but I believe life begins when the child is born."

"Gentlemen," said the rabbi, "you are both entitled to your opinion. But for a Jew, life begins when your son enters medical school."

*　　*　　*

Dobson, a gold prospector, walked Into an Organ Transplant Center and said to the doctor in charge, "I'd like to buy a vagina."

"That's a very unusual request. May I ask why?"

"Well," said Dobson, "I'm goin' up to Alaska to a real out-a-the-way spot where there won't be no woman. Now what 'aya got?"

"You're in luck" retorted the doctor. We just received the snatch of a 16-year-old Mexican gal. She'd been diddled only by three or four gangs. It'll cost you $1,000."

"Got anything better'n that?" asked Dobson.

"In the freezer we've got the box of a 26-year-old Irish Catholic nun. It was used only with Rosary beads—and once in a while, a crucifix—you can have that for $5,000."

"What's the best thing you got?"

"If you really want to go first class," said the M.D., "I can give you the twat of a 68-year-old woman who's traveled all over the world and was married for more than 40 years. That one is $50,000."

"You got a Mexican gal for $1,000, an Irish nun for $5,000 and you want $50,000 for some old cooze. How come?"

"Well," said the doctor, "this is the pussy of a Jewish Princess and it's never been used."

*   *   *

What is the difference between circumcision and crucifixion?

In circumcision they don't throw the whole Jew away.

* * *

ANCIENT JEWISH PROVERB

*A Jewish wife will forgive and forget
But she'll never forget what she forgave.*

* * *

Why does a Jewish Princess have crow's feet in the corners of her eyes?

From saying: "You want me to suck what?"

* * *

What is the first thing a Jewish Princess does with her asshole in the morning?

Sends him off to work.

* * *

What do you get if you cross a Jewish Princess and a hooker?

A girl who goes down on credit cards.

* * *

How does a Jewish Princess do it doggie style?

First, she makes her husband get down on all fours . . . then she rolls over and plays dead.

*   *   *

Paula, a pretty college student doing a graduate paper on American Indians, was interviewing various members of a tribe. She approached a brave with a feather in his hair. "Why do you wear a feather in your hair?" she asked.

"Me screw one maiden in tribe."

Paula noticed another brave with two feathers in his hair and she asked him why. "Me screw two Indian maiden," he answered.

Just then the elderly, slightly deaf chief emerged from his teepee wearing his full length headdress. Paula approached him and asked, "What do all those feathers in your headdress mean?"

"Me screw all maidens and squaws in tribe."

The girl gasped, "That's hostile!"

"Horsestyle, dogstyle, me do everything," bragged the hard of hearing chief.

"Oh, dear!" cried Paula.

"No, deer!" said the chief. "Hole too high—run too fast!"

*   *   *

Berkowitz, 86, was sitting in a chair on the porch of the Sholom Retirement Home. A nurse stood nearby observing his every move. When Berkowitz began leaning all the way over on his left side, the nurse quickly pushed him back to an upright sitting position.

As Berkowitz leaned all the way to his right side, the nurse again straightened him out. This procedure went on most of the morning until Berkowitz's son came to visit him. "Well, pop, how do you like it here?"

"It's okay," said the old man, "but the damn nurse don't let me fart."

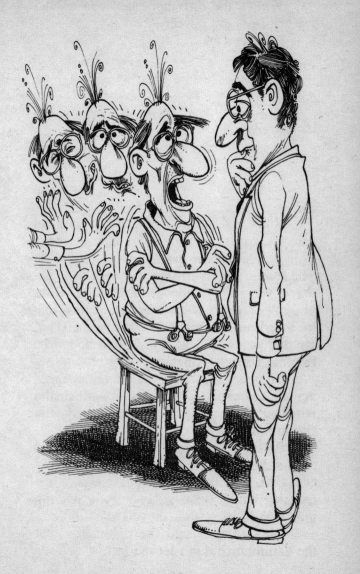

What's the difference between a Jewish Princess and poverty?

Poverty sucks.

*   *   *

Did you hear about the new Jewish Princess disease?

It's called MAIDS.

*   *   *

Running Deer walked into a small-town saloon carrying a bucket of manure and a little cat. Stuck in his belt was a six-gun. The Indian summoned the bartender and ordered whiskey. When he downed it, Running Deer ordered another. He drank that then ordered one more. When he finished, the Indian pulled out his six-gun and fired into the bucket of manure.

The cat jumped out of his arms, raced across the bar and all over room until finally Running Deer caught it, and returned with the animal under his arm.

"Hey," shouted the bartender, "what in hell do you think you're doin'?"

"Me just like white man," replied the Indian. "Have a few drinks, shoot the shit and chase a little pussy."

*   *   *

Did you hear about the Mexican who divorced his wife to marry a garbage can?

The hole was smaller and it smelled better!

* * *

In the early west, pioneers soon learned that some Indian tribes had very strange customs. One tribe made the youngest boys assume the roles, clothing, and customs of women, and take a brave for a husband. Part of this ritual involved a symbolic birth whereby the boys in drag defecate into a blanket and bury it, claiming that the baby had died.

Travers, a trapper passing through the territory of this tribe, spent the winter there and took one of the boys for his ''wife.'' In the spring, Travers left for the western range.

When he returned to the tribe six months later, Travers was accused of being the father of a child. He was taken to the chief's teepee, where the boy he'd been boffing all winter produced a blanket-papoose that turned out to be a blanket full of ca-ca. The chief looked at it carefully and said, ''You, Trapper! You leave Half-Nut after giving her baby. No doubt you father. Resemblance never lie.''

* * *

What is a plick?

A guy who doesn't leave a tip in a Chinese restaurant.

* * *

Machomania

An Insurance salesman said to Dalton, "How about signing up for a straight life policy?"

"Not just yet," said the macho mechanic. "Tell you the truth, I'm not ready for the straight life—I still like to step out once in a while."

*　*　*

*   *   *

Christine, a.very well-stacked brunette, was taking her driver's-license test. Suddenly, she felt the examiner's hand slide over her knees, and slip inside an intimate section of her anatomy. Surprised and angered, Christine stopped the car and slapped the man's face.

"Excellent reflexes," said the examiner. "By maintaining control of yourself, you have passed the test!"

*   *   *

There was a young fellow named Brett
Who made love in a car to Annette;
   It seems almost absurd,
   But the last that's been heard
They hadn't untangled them yet.

*   *   *

A pretty policewoman on the vice squad participated in her first bust on a house of ill-repute. She grabbed Lester, one of the horny young studs, and immediately read him his rights: "Anything you say will be held against you!"

And Lester screamed: "You! You! You!"

*   *   *

"Do you know what a guy with a 14-inch beef stick has for breakfast?" asked Craig.

"No!" replied his buddy Ben.

"This morning I had Wheaties, orange juice, bacon and eggs. . . ."

*   *   *

At a cocktail party, Victor had eyes for a luscious stewardess but she kept ignoring him. He finally grabbed her and said, "I can do things to you you've never had done in your life!"

"Like what?" asked the curious girl.

"I could drive you out of your mind with my tongue!"

"Oh, really?"

"Yeah," said Victor, "my tongue is so great, I could lick your belly button."

"What's so great about that?"

"From the inside?"

*   *   *

RELATIVE HUMIDITY

The sweat on your brow when you're humping your sister-in-law, and your wife's due back any minute

*   *   *

An older apartment dweller on Manhattan's East Side remarked to a neighbor,

"With all the male singles moving in, this building is going condom!"

*   *   *

Rick walked into an Atlantic City hotel men's room, and proceeded to relieve himself at the urinal. Suddenly, the man standing beside him exclaimed, "Wow! That's the biggest dong I've ever seen. How big is it when it gets stiff?"

"Damned if I know," replied Rick, "it draws all my blood and I pass out every time."

*   *   *

At a Honolulu cocktail party, Jeff approached Flora, the feminist fanatic, and flat out propositioned her.

"Listen, buster," snapped Flora, "I've developed an immunity to being used by men as a casual sex object."

"That figures," sneered Jeff, "considering the number of times you've been innoculated."

*   *   *

"I can make my dick 12 inches long."
"How?"
"I just fold it in half."

*   *   *

Did you hear about the 55-year-old bachelor who woke up one morning feeling like a 21-year-old?

Unfortunately, he couldn't find one that early in the day.

*   *   *

A rape case was in progress in Orange County Court. Willard was on the witness stand. "He had her backed up against that wall," said Willard, "and he was screwin' her to. . . ."

"Mr. Willard," interrupted the Judge. "Please don't use the word 'screw' in this court. Say 'intercourse' instead."

"Intercourse?" asked Willard. "What's that, Judge?"

"It's a technicality of language you wouldn't know anything about," said the Judge. "Proceed."

"Well, he had her up against that wall and he was intercoursin' 'er and suddenly he give her what we call the Louisville stroke, and she . . ."

"Wait a minute," said the judge. "What is the Louisville stroke?"

"That's a technicality of screwin', yer Honor, that you wouldn't know anythin' about."

*   *   *

Chuck Goldy, the Beverly Hills Volvo sales champ, gets chortles with this nifty joke:

Jarman was considered a bit eccentric but a brilliant inventor. He used his apartment as a laboratory. One day he was showing his friend Barney around.

They stopped in front of a red velvet curtain. With a flourish, Jarman pulled it back. There, stretched out on a bed, was a beautiful nude brunette. In her hand she held a glass, empty, except for two ice cubes.

"This is my latest invention," announced Jarman. "I call it instant sex. You just add Scotch."

Perry was sitting in a Beverly Hills health-club dining room, regaling his pals with tales of some girl he picked up the night before. "She was the musical type," he said smiling.

"What do you mean?" asked a buddy.

"Well, you know, she was fit as a fiddle and tight as a drum."

* * *

Arnold came on strong to Laura, but she was a liberated lady.

"All you guys have your brains between your legs!" she snapped.

"Yes!" he admitted. "And that gives me a mind-blowing idea!"

* * *

PERFECT LOVER

*A guy with a nine-inch tongue
who can breathe through his ears*

* * *

Archie and Marvin were off in the corner observing the office-party celebrants. "Wait a minute," challenged Archie. "How can you tell Rita ain't wearing no pants?"

"Easy," said Marvin, "can't you see the dandruff all over her suede shoes?"

A medical school professor was lecturing to his class. "This is the skull of a young man, a weight lifter, who was shipwrecked for six months on a desert island with five cocktail waitresses."

A future M.D. muttered, "What was the cause of death?"

*   *   *

Denby, in his early twenties, was confiding to the family physician. "I've only had one erection in my life."

"That is a problem," said the M.D. "How long was its duration?"

Well, the fellow thought, *I was fifteen at the time and I'm now twenty three . . .* "That makes it eight years!" he said.

*   *   *

"Hey, Tony, heard you went discoing Saturday night. How was it?"

"The joint was jammed. The dance floor was so crowded I was dancing cheek to cheek with the girl behind me."

*   *   *

What is the height of rejection?

When you're masturbating and it goes limp.

*   *   *

Dr. Andrews was discussing masturbation as a possible temporary therapeutic practice with his patient Jensen. "But I already derive pleasure from my own organ, doctor," said Jensen. "I frequently grasp my penis and hold it firmly. It's a habit with me."

"In that case," said the M.D., "it's a habit you'll have to shake."

* * *

Owen was seeking advice from Payton, a wise old bachelor. "How do you really feel about the ladies?"

"Every man should have a girl for love, companionship, and sympathy," said Payton, "preferably at three different addresses."

* * *

"You mean you stopped drinking just because she asked you to?"

"Yes."

"And you gave up cigarettes for the same reason?"

"That's right."

"And you stopped gambling and racing cars just for her?"

"I did."

"Then, after all that, why didn't you marry her?"

"Well, I figured I'd become such a nice, clean-cut guy that I could do better."

*   *   *

Agatha and Jerry met at a singles' bar, and were heading for her apartment when an icy wind came up.

"Br-r-r!" said Agatha. "Do you know what the forecast is?"

"The prediction is for better than six inches," replied Jerry, "and, it might even snow."

*   *   *

A Texas millionaire was introduced to a Las Vegas showgirl, and it was love at first sight. The next evening he proposed marriage.

"Tell you what," she said. "I'll marry you on three conditions. You gotta get me a custom-built Rolls Royce. Second, put five million dollars in the bank in my name. And then guarantee me that you'll give me twelve inches of tallywhacker."

"Lemme git busy on it, honey," said the Texan.

The following day he returned. "Here," he said, "is the bill of sale for the Rolls. Here's your deposit slip for the five million. And here is a guarantee signed by the best surgeon at Sunrise Hospital saying he'll cut it down to whatever size you want."

*   *   *

Henderson had no arms. He walked up to a bar and asked for a beer. The bartender placed a glass of suds in front of him.

"Look," said the customer, "I have no arms—would you please hold the glass up to my mouth?"

"Sure," said the bartender.

"Now," said Henderson, "could you get the handkerchief out of my pocket and wipe the foam off my mouth."

"Certainly."

"If," said the armless man, "you'd reach in my righthand pants' pocket, you'll find the money for the beer."

The bartender got it.

"You been real nice," said Henderson. "Just one thing more. Where is the men's room?"

"Out the door," said the bartender, "turn right, walk three blocks, and there's one in a filling station on the corner."

There once was a flasher named Saul
Who stationed himself in a mall.
   He unzipped as he bowed
   To the curious crowd,
Then extended his welcome to all.

*   *   *

Did you hear about the window washer on the tenth floor of the Empire State Building who suddenly appeared at a window and frightened an executive out of his secretary?

*   *   *

Hank: Why don't women have hair on their chests?

Glen: Did you ever see grass grow on a playground?

*   *   *

Rudy met Harriet at a Staten Island singles' dance. When he learned she was a virgin, he refused to deflower her. "But," he said, "we could definitely get it on after you're no longer a virgin."

"I see," sneered Harriet, "you want somebody else to do all the dirty work, and then you'll take all the pleasure."

"Sure," replied Rudy. "Just because I didn't dig the subway, doesn't mean I don't ride in it!"

BRAD'S BIBLICAL BROMIDE
Thou shalt not covet thy neighbor's wife,
His ass thou shalt not slaughter.
But thank your stars it isn't a sin
To covet thy neighbor's daughter.

*   *   *

CONFIRMED BACHELOR

*A man who goes through life without
a hitch*

*   *   *

The clothing flew in every direction as the swingers started getting belted with booze. As the orgy started, a tall, stacked, honey-haired nurse walked up to Zack. She glanced at his somewhat limited natural endowment, then laughed. "And just who do you think you're gonna please with *that*?"

"Me!" replied Zack.

*   *   *

In the Garden of Eden lay Adam
Complacently stroking his madam,
    And loud was his mirth
    For he knew that on earth
There were only two balls—and he had 'em.

85

TO: ALL MALE TAXPAYERS
FROM: INTERNAL REVENUE SERVICE
DATE: APRIL 1, 1984

Dear Taxpayers:

The only good thing that the Internal Revenue has not taxed is your pecker. This is due to the fact that 40% of the time it is hanging around unemployed, 30% of the time it is pissed, 20% of the time it is hard-up, and 10% of the time it is employed, but it operates in a hole. Furthermore, it has two dependents and they are both nuts.

Accordingly, after September 1, 1984 your pecker will be taxed on its size, using the "Pecker-Checker" scale below. Determine your category and insert the additional tax under "Other Taxes," page 2 Part V, line C-1 of your standard income tax return (Form 1040).

PECKER-CHECKER SCALE

10-12 inches. . .Luxury Tax $30.00
8-9   inches. . .Hole Tax 25.00
6-7   inches. . .Privilege Tax 15.00
4-5   inches. . .Nuisance Tax 5.00

NOTE: Anyone with a pecker under 4 inches is eligible for refund.

DO NOT APPLY FOR AN EXTENSION

Males with peckers in excess of 12 inches should file under "Capital Gains."

Very truly yours,

Peter J. Cutchapeckeroff

*　　*　　*

Mark, a rich Bel Air kid, was cruising in his new Mazaratti trying to pick up a girl. That night a friend asked how he made out that day. "Nothing!" replied Mark dejectedly.

"You got the wrong car to pick up chicks. Get a van."

He did. Next Mark picked up a blonde on Sunset Boulevard. They drove off into a secluded spot and made it big in back of the van. "You do anything else?" asked Mark.

"Sure," answered the girl.

"Let's have it all, baby!"

The girl got out of the van, ripped off the radio aerial and climbed back in. She had Mark lie on his stomach and began whipping him with the aerial.

Next day Mark woke up black and blue with welts all over his body. He rushed to the doctor's office and pulled off his clothes. "Gee, doc," he whined "please tell me what I've got."

After a quick look the doctor replied, "Son, that's the worst case of van-aerial disease I've ever seen."

*　　*　　*

Did you hear about the guy who was so well endowed that he had a fiveskin?

*　　*　　*

Neville had been imbibing vodka gimlets at a Cleveland bar most of the night. Feeling no pain, he turned to the girl sitting next to him and muttered, ''Wanna screw?''

She slapped Neville in the face, knocking him off the bar stool.

Neville got up, brushed himself off, and returned to his seat. After another gimlet he looked at the girl again and said, ''Why don't we go out tonight and screw?''

This time she grabbed a beer bottle, hit him over the head, and again he fell to the floor.

Neville looked up at the girl and asked, ''I suppose a blow job is out of the question?''

Eileen and Dan met at a birthday party. Twenty minutes later they had locked the bathroom door behind them and were petting in a frenzy.

"What does your father do for a living?" panted Dan.

"He's a bill-poster!" said Eileen.

"Well . . . here comes some paste for him."

*   *   *

A shipwrecked sailor, who had spent many years on a remote South Pacific island, was finally rescued.

When he arrived in San Diego, reporters asked him what he had done for sex.

"Oh, there were plenty of passable and willing native girls on the island," he replied, "but they all had either V.D. or T.B."

"That must have been frustrating," commented one of the newsmen.

"Not really," said the sailor. "If a girl coughed, I screwed her."

*   *   *

Trevor, a biology teacher, was undressing his willing, voluptuous, teenage student. "Of course you know," she giggled, "that I am not at the age of consent?"

"Never mind," he gasped, "tomorrow you can bring a note from your mother."

*   *   *

Miss Barish, a spinsterish prude, sat next to a sophisticated stud at a formal dinner. Their conversation was strained. Finally the lady said, "It's quite obvious that we do not agree on a single, solitary thing."

"Oh, that's not true, Ma'am," said the young swinger. "Let me ask you this, if you walked into a bedroom where there were two beds, and if there was a woman in one and a man in the other, in which bed would you sleep?"

"Obviously," snapped Miss Barish, "with the woman."

"You see, we agree," said the dude. "So would I."

* * *

We know three nice gals out at Huxham,
And whenever we meet 'em, we fucks 'em.
 But when that game gets stale,
  We all sit on a rail
And pull out our pricks and they sucks 'em.

* * *

Doug and Gordon met in the locker room after a racquetball game at the YMCA. "I'll bet you $100 I'm longer soft than you are hard," said Doug.

"You got a bet. How long are you soft?"

"About three years."

*   *   *

George, who had a penis that was eighteen inches long, wanted to join the Long Dick Club. He asked a guy who belonged to propose him for membership. The member turned back the lapel of his overcoat. "See that flower in my button hole?"

"Yeah."

"Well, that's the head of my pecker, and I'm only the doorman."

*   *   *

Lambert was working on the 30th floor of a new skyscraper when he felt the need to pee. "Can I go down to the toilet?" he asked the foreman.

"With the kind of money we're paying you guys, it'll take too long," replied the foreman. "Put a plank over the edge of the steel section, walk out on the end, I'll stand on this end, and you can relieve yourself. By the time it hits the first floor it'll disappear."

That's what they did. Lambert stood out on the end of the wooden plank, the foreman balancing it. But the phone rang. Instinctively the foreman left to answer it, and Lambert left for the concrete thirty stories below.

The foreman took the elevator down to see what happened, but was stopped by a workingman on the eighth floor. "Hey," he screamed, "what kind of perverts you got working on this job?"

"What're you talking about?" asked the foreman.

"Some guy just came flying by here holding his prick yelling, 'Where did that cocksucker go?'"

Hookermania

Daphne, Sabina, and Erica were discussing their johns.

"I can't stand these guys with little peckers," complained Daphne, "you got to roll up into a ball to take it."

"Yeah," agreed Sabina, "but it's not good when they're too long either. What I like is when they're really stubby and thick, like a baby's fist."

Erica said nothing, and finally the other two asked her, "Well, what kind of pricks do you like best?"

"What the hell does it matter?" she replied. "They all taste alike, don't they?"

*   *   *

HOSE

Prostitutes from the deep south

*   *   *

Said a dainty young whore named Miss Meggs,
"The men like to spread my two legs,
    Then slip in between
    If you know what I mean,
And leave me the white of their eggs."

*   *   *

Fletcher came from a small midwestern town to work in New York City. A year later a friend visited him and asked, "How do you like it here?"

"I live in a real swell neighborhood near Park Avenue," replied Fletcher. "When I come home at night, you ought to see all the beautiful women. They're dressed up so swell and look so nice, you would never take them for whores!"

*   *   *

A hillbilly visiting his first whorehouse began laughing when he saw the prostitute's vagina.

"You shouldn't laugh," she said, "you came out of one of those."

"Yeah," he said, "but that's the first one ah ever seed that ah could climb back into."

*   *   *

Did you hear about the call girl who got tired of spending all her time in bed, so she settled for a desk job?

* * *

Ernie was very pleased with the pretty massage-parlor attendant. "You're so young," he said. "You must have a lot of experience to be so good at your work."

"I started last Monday," she replied.

"Really?" said horny Ernie. "What did you do before?"

"I had a job on a dairy farm milking cows."

* * *

Business was booming at the local whorehouse, and this particular night they were short-handed. Penelope was going down on a customer, and the madam kept knocking on the door and hurrying the girl, who kept answering in a muffled voice, "I'll be right ouououout!"

At the third interruption, the man shouted, "You heard her! She'll be right out! And as for you, quit using my dick for a telephone!"

* * *

Why is a prostitute like a police station? Dicks are always going in and out.

A homely young harlot named Gert
Used to streetwalk until her corns hurt;
   But now she just stands
   Upside down on her hands,
With her face covered up by her skirt.

*   *   *

Stanton, in Portland on business, picked up Jelena in the hotel bar and took her up to his room. After a few drinks the girl sat on his lap. "Would you like to hug me." she asked.

"Sure," said Stanton, pulling her close.

"And would you like to kiss me?" asked Jelena.

"Of course," replied Stanton, placing his tongue deep in her mouth.

"Okay, honey," she continued, "brace yourself, because here comes the 100 dollar question."

*   *   *

Randy and Wade, two automobile salesmen, were having a drink at a Detroit bar. "I've often wondered why they call hookers 'ladies of the evening'?"

"Well, did you ever see one in the daylight?"

*   *   *

A rookie cop came out of a bawdy house and ran into his sergeant. The young police officer smoothed his hair, fixed his tie, and said, "It's okay, Sarge, I paid for it!"

"I don't care if you did pay your way!" shouted his superior. "I wasn't suggesting you were on the take. It just doesn't look right for you to go over my head by doing business with the Chief's wife."

*　　*　　*

A naked young tart named Roselle
Walked the streets while ringing a bell.
　　When asked why she rang it,
　　She answered, "Gol dang it!
Can't you see I have something to sell?"

*　　*　　*

OBESE HOOKER

A roly holer

*　　*　　*

After a blow job, Howard said to the call girl, "How 'bout an old-fashioned bang?"

"Forget it!" she sid angrily. "I'm saving that for Mr. Right!"

*　　*　　*

Fowler telephoned a Manhattan call-girl service and said to the madam, "I want the skinniest, scrawniest babe you got."

"Sure," replied the madam. "Got just what you want. Name's Dorinda. I'll send her over."

Thirty minutes later, the emaciated prostitute arrived. The girl was so thin she could have been a model for x-rays. "Go into the bedroom and take off your clothes," said Fowler.

She obeyed.

"Now get down on your hands and knees."

Dorinda did as beckoned. Suddenly, Fowler left the room and returned with a terribly skinny dog.

Fowler pointed to the hooker and then said to the animal, "See, Dixie, if you don't eat, that's what you're gonna look like."

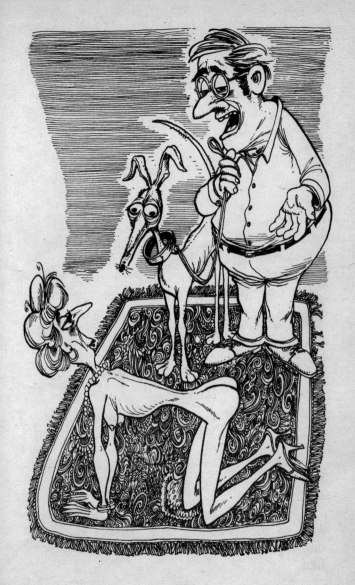

What do you get when you cross a hooker and a Chinaman?

A girl who sucks laundry.

* * *

BROTHEL

*A house where the madam in charge
offers vice to the lovelorn*

* * *

Jennifer asked Whitman what he wanted.

"What's your specialty?" he asked.

"Well," she said, "my prices are $10, $20, $50, and $100, and you can take your pick. I'll jerk you off, suck you off, screw you off, or take out my glass eye and wink you off!"

* * *

Cheryl left the profession, and was beating the drum for the Salvation Army on a busy street corner:

"Yes, once I lay in the arms of men. White men! Black men! Chinamen! Yes, I lay in the arms of the devil!"

"That's right, sister," came a voice from the rear. "Screw 'em all!"

* * *

Clinton offered a street walker $500 if she'd let him do what he wanted to her. The prostie led him to her apartment and said, "All right, honey, what do you want to do?"

"I need to crap on your face!"

The prostitute stared for a moment, thought of the huge amount of money and then agreed. The next night Clinton returned, paid her $500, and proceeded to relieve himself.

The next ten nights in a row, the same routine was repeated and then something happened. On the eleventh night Clinton squatted over the woman, grunted, and was unable to have a B.M. He looked down at the prostitute and saw that she had tears rolling down her cheeks.

"What are you crying for?" asked the john.

"You've been with another woman!" sobbed the streetwalker.

*   *   *

Angel ran into her friend Edwina. "Where ya been, hon. Ain't seen you 'round lately."

"After turning tricks for a year," said the streetwalker, "I finally decided to take a vacation in Vegas. And you know what? I lost all my fucking money!"

*   *   *

Madame Magdala was dumbfounded when a 14-year-old boy said he wanted one of her girls who was suffering from a dose of the clap. The madame obliged. Several weeks later she ran across the boy and asked him if he got what he requested.

"Sure," he bubbled, "but they gave me shots and I'm cured now."

"But why did you want to catch V.D.?" she asked.

"Well, it's kinda complicated. Before I went to the doctor, I gave the disease to the maid. She gave it to my father and, naturally, my mother got it next."

"But you didn't want to infect her?"

"Nah," replied the boy. "It's the milkman I was after. He's the bastard who ran over my bike."

* * *

One whore complained to the other that times were bad.

"You call this bad? Why I hear that in St. Louis they're sucking cocks for food!"

* * *

SIGN ON BROTHEL

Why be inches away from happiness?

* * *

In a Pennsylvania mining town a street-walker approached a miner. He told her he had no money at all on him, but asked if she would take him on for a dollar credit he had at a nearby restaurant.

She agreed to give him a blow job for the credit voucher, and knelt down on the ground before him. Just as she was clamping her mouth down on his penis, she stopped, looked up, and said out of one corner of her mouth, "Say, is that a clean place?"

*   *   *

Said a madam named Mamie La Farge
To a sailor just off of a barge,
    "We have one girl that's dead,
    With a hole in her head—
Of course there's a slight extra charge."

*   *   *

Alastair saw his father coming out of a notorious brothel.

"Father!" he shouted.

"Son," replied the father, "say nothing! I prefer the simulated enthusiasm of a paid prostitute to the dignified acquiescence of your mother."

*   *   *

105

Huntington rang the doorbell at Polly Adler's famous brothel, and Madam Adler responded, her mascara streaked, her eyes all puddled up.

"Is Krystal here?" asked Huntington.

"Oh," cried the celebrated madam, "Krystal died last night. We've got her laid out on a couch in there. Come on in and see the poor thing."

They walked into the parlor and there was the dead prostitute.

"God!" he exclaimed. "I hate to see Krystal lying cold in death like that! She was not only a good piece of ass—she was better at Frenchin' than any women I ever met!"

"That's the way with you goddamn men!" moaned Polly. "You never say a good word about anybody till they're dead!"

What is the four-letter word most frequently heard in a whorehouse?

"Next!"

*   *   *

Mrs. Anderson bought a parrot but could not get it to talk. The family tried everything, beginning with "Polly want a cracker?" but with no result. That afternoon at her bridge party, the discussion turned to the current quality of silk underwear.

"Look at this wonderful slip," said Mrs. Green turning up the corner of her dress.

"And look at these wonderful panties," said Mrs. Hall, pulling up her skirt all the way.

"Home at last," shouted the parrot. "One of you whores give me a cigarette."

*   *   *

Harrison, age 74, leaving his favorite prostitute, said, "See you again in three months."

"You old reprobate," she chided. "Don't you ever think of anything but pussy?

*   *   *

What do you get when you cross a hooker with a computer?

A fucking know-it-all.

Madame Gabrielle had Melissa in her office.

"I could understand your falling asleep on the job," railed the madam, "but falling asleep on a blow job. . . !"

* * *

On a busy night at the cat house, several men sat downstairs waiting their turns. Osborn pulled his collar up around his neck and muttered, "My wife would beat me up if she knew where I was."

"That's nothing," said Skelly. "My wife would kill me."

"I don't care who knows I come here," said Norton, "because I'm a bachelor."

"So if you're not married," asked Osborn, "how come you have to go out and buy a piece?"

* * *

Wanda and Angelique, two Park Avenue prosties, were having a late drink.

"How come you never married," asked Wanda.

"I got nothing against marriage," answered Angelique. "Some of my best friends are husbands."

* * *

PROSTITUTION

Fee love

* * *

Did you hear about the whore in the leper colony?

She did all right till her business dropped off.

* * *

He was a slob, but they let him in the Marty's Massage Parlor anyway. She was naive, and when he offered her 50 bucks to go all the way, the pretty masseuse smiled and agreed.

While they huffed and puffed, her boss walked into the cubicle, took a look at what was going on, and said, "What's a joint like that doing in a nice girl like you?"

* * *

The ladies who ply their trade on Broadway were envious of the success of Margo, an old and bedraggled whore.

They tried time and again to learn the secret of her success. They plied her with drink, they flattered her, they begged her, they cajoled her, and they even threatened her. But she wouldn't reveal what made her so popular.

Finally they lost patience and ganged up on her in an alleyway. Just as a stocky Black was about to thump her, the old lady shouted, "All right, I give in!"

"Tell us, then," exclaimed the attackers.

"It's like this," said Margo. "I give Green Stamps."

*   *   *

Peggy, a poor Polish girl from Pennsylvania, traveled to Hollywood, and in a very short time made it big in the massage-parlor world.

Her girlfriends proudly proclaimed that Peggy had gone from *rags* to *rigids*.

*   *   *

What do the cops call teenage delinquents they pick up in bawdy houses?

Brothel sprouts!

*   *   *

Corrine was fed up with the Cleveland winters and decided to move to Florida. Within a few weeks she became enormously popular in Miami and Miami Beach. Down in citrusland she is now famous as "The Tail of Two Cities."

*   *   *

One summer morning, young Calvin went to his father and said, "Dad, I ain't got nothin' to do."

His father thought it might be a good idea to keep the boy busy by sending him on a wild-goose chase. He handed the youngster a bill and said, "Here, son, go get me a dollar's worth of What's What."

Calvin hurried down to the town drugstore and said to the owner, "I need a dollar's worth of What's What."

The druggist knew immediately the boy was being sent on a wild-goose chase. "I don't have any," he said, "but why don't you try the house over there with the red light on it. They'll have some."

Calvin rushed over to the bawdy house and knocked on the door. A six-foot blonde, stark naked, opened the door and her crotch was right in the boy's face. "What's that?" he asked.

"What's what?" asked the girl.

"Give me a dollar's worth!" said the boy.

Said the prostitute to the plastic surgeon: "C'mon, Doc, make it snappy."

*　　*　　*

"Absolutely not, Mr. Donaldson," said the hooker to one of her regular customers. "No more credit. You're in to me for too much already."

*　　*　　*

SIGN ON A BROTHEL DOOR

Out to lunch—Go Screw Yourself

*　　*　　*

Donald found himself unable to "touch bottom" while making it with a prostitute.

"Can't you do something about this?" he said. "It's like waving a flag in space."

The woman was insulted and invited him to examine her vagina. Donald probed and stared and suddenly lost his footing and fell in. He wandered for a while, and finally met a man with a lantern. "How do you get out of here?" asked Donald.

"I don't know," said the man. "I've been here two weeks looking for a team of horses."

*　　*　　*

Said an elderly whore named Maureen,
"I prefer a young lad of eighteen.
There's more cream in his larder,
And his pecker gets harder,
And he screws in a manner obscene."

*   *   *

On making his first trip to Kansas City, Stillman found the most luxurious bordello in town. He selected a luscious blonde, and was escorted to a bedchamber that looked like it belonged in a Beverly Hills mansion.

Half an hour later, he went to the madam and prepared to pay her. But the madam would not accept payment. In fact, she handed him $100.

A week later he returned, chose a succulent redhead and was presented with $200 by the madam.

The next night he went back again. After enjoying a beautiful brunette, he walked up to the madam, held out his hand, and waited for the money.

"That'll be fifty dollars, please," said the madam.

"Wait a minute," said Stillman, "the first time you gave me a hundred dollars. Next time, you gave me two hundred dollars. How come I didn't get paid tonight?"

"Tonight," replied the madam, "you were not on Cable TV!"

Show Bizmania

Jenny had been in Hollywood only a week, when she wound up in a motel with a big producer.

"No kidding? Mr. Ross," said Jenny. "Do I really have a chance of becoming a big star?"

"Honey," said Ross, glancing downward, "you're already making it big."

* * *

A famous movie mogul was having difficulty persuading a young starlet to go home and listen to his stereo. "Look," he implored, "how long have I known you?"

"About three quarters of an hour," she replied.

"All right, then!" he declared. "Have I ever lied to you?"

* * *

Barney, the agent for a beautiful actress, found out she'd been selling her body for $100 a night.

Barney told her he wanted to make it with her. She agreed to spend the night with him, but said he'd have to pay her the same $100 that the other customers did.

"Don't I even get my agent's 10% as a deduction?"

"No, baby," she said. "You want it, you gotta pay full price!"

Barney agreed and that night she came to his apartment. He turned out all the lights and screwed her till midnight.

At 1 A.M. she was awakened again and vigorously screwed. In a little while, she was roused once more and screwed again. The actress was impressed with her lover's vitality.

"My God!" she whispered in the dark. "You are virile. I never realized how lucky I was to have you as my agent."

"I'm not your agent, lady," said a strange voice. "He's at the door selling tickets!"

Did you hear about the sentimental movie star who wants to get divorced in the same dress in which her mother got divorced?

* * * *

TINSEL TOWN TALE

No matter how much money a Hollywood producer has, he can't resist making a little extra on the side.

* * *

An actor met a pretty actress while filming a TV sitcom on the Universal lot.

"How about it?" he proposed. "Let's get married."

"No," she answered, "I'm afraid I can't."

"Aw, why not," he pleaded. "It's just for a few days!"

* * *

A starlet managed to get a date with a top producer. She returned from the date with spirits high and reported to her roommate, "We're off to a great start. I said 'no' to him from the minute we climbed into his car. He kept asking, 'Do you mind if I do this?' and 'Do you mind if I do that?' "

* * *

At the Bistro, two actors were discussing another actor who just got himself engaged to an actress.

"She's a nice girl," they agreed. "She'll make him a marvelous first wife!"

* * *

"I finally figured out what they mean when some movies are advertised as having a *star studded* cast."

"What?"

"It means the actresses not only had to sleep with the producer, they got it from the leading man, too."

* * *

STARLET

In Hollywood, any girl under thirty who is not regularly employed in a brothel

* * *

On the movie set the producer thundered for the imported director, "Where the hell is that Italian cocksucker, Bongavani?"

"Please!" shouted the director. "French cocksucker."

* * *

121

Willis and Kent, a much out-of-work vaudeville dance team, arrived in Newark for an audition. The men were very nervous because Carlton, the theater manager, had a peculiar way of judging performers. He had an owl perched on the balcony. During the audition, if the owl winked his right eye, the act was not hired. In addition, Carlton was a notorious ladies' man and Willis had a pretty wife.

But Willis and Kent, desperately in need of a job, went out on the stage while the owl was on the balcony rail. In a minute, Willis noticed the manager in the wings, wrapping his arms around his pretty wife.

"Jesus," said Willis under his breath. "That son of a bitch Carlton is fooling around with my wife."

Kent whispered, "Just keep going."

Kent kept dancing. But Willis kept looking and then he saw that the manager had his. . . .

"For Christ's sake!" Willis whispered. "That bastard is screwing my wife!"

And Kent whispered back, "Never mind that! Watch that fuckin' owl!"

*　　*　　*

Auditions were being held for a new T.V. variety show. Franklin, a Black truck driver, showed up and claimed that he could sing through his ass. The producer was impressed with the uniqueness of the talent, and asked the man to demonstrate.

Franklin dropped his trousers and shorts, and then he proceeded to move his bowels on the floor.

The producer screamed, "What the hell are you doing?"

The Black man replied, "I'm just clearing my throat."

*   *   *

There once was a sperm named Herm who lived inside a famous movie actor. Herm was a very healthy sperm. He'd do push-ups and somersaults and limber himself up all the time, while the other sperm just lay around on their fat asses not doing a thing.

One of them became curious enough to ask Herm why he exercised all day.

"Look," said Herm, "only one sperm gets a woman pregnant and, when the right time comes, I am going to be that one."

A few days later, they all felt themselves getting hotter and hotter, and they knew that it was getting to be their time to go. They were released abruptly and, sure enough, Herm was swimming far ahead of all the others.

All of a sudden, Herm stopped, turned around, and began to swim back with all his might. "Go back! Go back!" he screamed. "It's just a blow job!"

123

Did you hear about the incredibly well-hung porno actor whose star is rising?

*   *   *

A young leading man named McCall,
Consistently practiced withdrawal.
　　This quaint predilection
　　Created such friction
He soon had no foreskin at all.

*   *   *

The male member of a mind-reading act was bragging about his recent engagement.

"Do you know," he boasted, "I guessed what object my partner was holding up every time, without her giving me a clue."

"That's great!"

"Not really," said the mind reader, "we were performing in a male nudist camp."

*   *   *

OVERHEARD ON MOVIE SET

Director: Now here's the scene where you jump off the cliff.

Actor: Yeah, but suppose I get killed?

Director: Don't worry. It's the last scene in the picture.

"What's new on Broadway?"

"Same old stuff. A showgirl just wrote her memoirs and confessed that she had been unsuccessful in show biz until she had her 'no's' fixed."

* * *

Toward the end of her career, Ethel Barrymore starred in a new play on Broadway. Out of respect for her age, she was permitted to sit in the wings, knitting during rehearsals while an understudy did her scenes.

Also in the cast was a voluptuous young blonde who had a walk-on part because she was a "friend" of the play's principal backer. She had no talent, but she was shrewd, and soon she was in bed with the director, who agreed to let her speak one line. Then, after getting the playwright into the hay, she got four more lines. By this time the producer began asking, "What's the matter? Don't I like pussy?" He was quickly laid and the blonde wound up with the whole scene.

After each of these triumphs, she had gone to Miss Barrymore to tell her the good news. Now, once again, she appeared in the presence of the great star.

"They've given me a whole scene!" she gushed. "Will you watch me rehearse and tell me what you think?"

"Of course," said Miss Barrymore. "But just remember, my dear. You can't screw the audience."

(The curtain rises to reveal)

Scene I

(A darkened hotel room. The only illumination is provided by a sign outside the window that continually blinks on and off. During those intervals when the external light leaks into the room, we see a couple sitting on the bed, almost fully clothed.)

WALT: *(tenderly)* Ah, come on, Honey, just say you will. There's nothing to it.

GAIL: *(hesitatingly)* Well, I suppose . . . all right!

Then
Scene II

(Same. A few hours later.)

WALT: *(proudly)* Well, how was it?

GAIL: *(sarcastically)* You were right. There's nothing to it.

(Blackout)

*   *   *

Once upon a time there was a ventriloquist who was so bad you could see his lips move even when he wasn't saying anything.

*   *   *

Did you hear about the ventriloquist who talked in his sleep?

His wife had to go into the next room to hear what he was saying.

*   *   *

In Tinsel Town these days the hottest property is the new Hawaiian star Kuna Cole. She makes many skin flicks and the work is extremely exhausting. So for some of the scenes she uses a lie-in.

*   *   *

Madden had a job helping the veterinary in the circus. His specialty was blowing obstructions out of the elephant's ass with a straw. Madden's friends pleaded with him that this was a terrible job, and that he surely could find something better. "What!" he cried, "you want me to leave show business!"

*   *   *

A film star far gone in lechery
Lured girls to their doom by his treachery.
　　He invited them in
　　For the purpose of sin,
Though he said 'twas to look at his etchery.

*　　*　　*

The circus was coming to town. The elephants, all four of them, walked in traditional fashion, each one grasping with his trunk the tail of the elephant in front of him. They reached a train crossing and almost crossed it safely. A train came along, knocked down and killed the last elephant.

A few months later the railroad company received a bill for damages, including the loss of four elephants.

"But we only killed one elephant," said the spokesman.

"Yes," said the circus owner, "but you tore asses out of the other three."

*　　*　　*

SIDESHOW BARKER

"She's right here on the inside,
folks. Fatima, the famous dancing girl!
Why she dances on her left leg,
she dances on her right leg,
and between them she makes a living!"

*　　*　　*

During Vaudeville days, Eli and Flo were sitting in the dark near the front of the theater.

"Flo," whispered Eli, "keep on playing with it and making it bigger."

"All right," said the girl, "if you promise to control yourself, and not make a mess."

Eli promised, but she got him so aroused he broke his word.

"There!" snapped Flo. "Now you've come in my hand, what should I do with it?"

"Raise your hand and flip it away."

The girl did as she was told and flipped it away.

Down in the orchestra pit there was another whispered argument, between the conductor and the first fiddle.

"Hey, for cripes' sake, you're about three bars late!" growled the conductor.

"Well, somebody's come in my eye!" said the violinist.

"I'm not surprised, you've been playing like a twat all night."

* * *

There was a Vaudevillian named Sweeney
Whose girl was a terrible meanie.
   The hatch of her snatch
   Had a catch that would latch—
She could only be screwed by Houdini.

The Broadway chorus girl was exuberant over receiving a role in an upcoming play.

"I was made for the part," she exclaimed happily.

"Shhh," cautioned her roommate. "You don't have to tell everybody."

* * *

The dance band was playing a small town in the midwest, and was doing fine until somebody called the piccolo player a cocksucker. The leader's baton beat a tattoo on his music stand, and the musicians stopped playing. He turned to his audience. "Who called my piccolo player a cocksucker?" he demanded.

A voice in the rear of the hall yelled back, "Who called that cocksucker a piccolo player?"

* * *

During the orchestra rehearsal of a beautiful passage in Ravel's "Bolero," a homosexual clarinetist kept blowing the wrong note. He finally excused himself to the conductor. "I'm sorry. That passage moves me so much, instead of blowing, I suck."

* * *

A well-known Broadway leading man's adventures with the ladies cost him several jobs. One producer refused to permit him to enter his office.

Last summer the producer came up with a new play. The actor wanted to appear in it so desperately that he wrote him a letter, "I am through with women. Give me this part and I swear to you that during the entire run of the play I won't even let a female call me by my first name."

The producer relented and gave him the part. Rehearsals were to start in two days. But the next afternoon, the actor was walking down Broadway with a pretty woman he'd picked up an hour before, when he bumped into the producer.

"Don't jump to conclusions," said the actor, "I want you to meet my wife."

"Your wife!" roared the producer. "You bastard—she's *my* wife!"

There was a young actor named Moore,
Whose tool was a yard long or more,
So he wore the damn thing
In a surgical sling
To keep it from wiping the floor.

* * *

What's better than a rose on a piano?
Two lips on an organ.

* * *

What is ASCAP?
A Gay contraceptive.

* * *

Did you hear about the musician who worked all week on an arrangement, and then his wife didn't go out of town after all?

* * *

An actor leaving a pay toilet notices that the attendant is a former theatrical star. "Oh my," he said, as he dropped a dollar in the tip plate. "You must be starving to do this."

"Oh, it isn't as bad as all that," said the former star. "Of course, business has been a little slow this morning. I've had twelve pissers, and you're the third shit to come in."

The big Hollywood producer left the studio and drove to his huge Bel Air mansion. Upon arriving at the house, he found his wife sobbing uncontrollably.

"Good heavens, what's the matter?" he asked.

"That famous Broadway playwright you just signed," she wailed, "he came marching in this afternoon, seized me in his arms, and despite my protests, made violent love to me for three hours."

"Hmmm," mused the producer, "I wonder what the so-and-so wants?"

*　　*　　*

At a Los Angeles party, Boswell boasted that he was endowed with a wondrous sense of smell. Just one sniff in the dark, and he could tell what the object was.

The host and his guests decided to put him to the test. An assortment of twigs were brought into the room, and Boswell was blindfolded.

One of the twigs was held under his nose for an instant. "Pine," said the wizard.

Another twig Boswell guessed to be birch, another oak, another hickory, and so on—all correctly.

To further test the powers, a guy who had just come from a sex orgy held his forefinger under the expert's nose.

"Hollywood," declared Boswell.

"There's a fella lives on my block who used to work in the circus by putting his right arm into the lion's mouth."

"What's his name?"

"I don't know, but we all call him 'Lefty.' "

* * *

Millard, a stockbroker, stopped off at a piano bar for a drink. He ordered a Rob Roy on the rocks and listened to the song being played. He thought it was truly beautiful. When the pianist finished Millard said, "That was the most beautiful song I've ever heard."

"Thank you," said the piano player. "I wrote it about a year ago."

"Really? I've never heard it."

"You wouldn't. It never sold."

"That's too bad," offered Millard. "It's such a wonderful tune."

"Yeah," agreed the pianist, "they liked the music okay but they wouldn't go for the title and I wouldn't change it."

"That's ridiculous!" said the stockbroker. "What difference does the title make? It's the song that's important."

"I know," said the piano player, "but they didn't want the title I had for it."

"For heaven's sake, what's the title?"

"I Love You So Damn Much My Balls Ache."

Matrimonymania

On the first night of their honeymoon, Norbert turned to Marcia and said, "Honey, I'm really nuts about you."

"I'm glad you feel that way, darling," she purred, " 'cause there's something I've been meaning to tell you."

"Yeah?"

"I used to be a topless waitress."

"That's awful! I'd rather have married a hooker."

"Eh . . . there was another thing I forgot to tell you. . . ."

* * *

Harley and Blanche were up in their honeymoon room and were getting ready for bed. Blanche took off all her clothes quickly, and waited patiently for her husband.

He removed his shoes then turned away. "Why are you hiding your feet?"

"I've got toetinitis."

Harley then removed his pants and once again turned around so Blanche wouldn't see his knees. "What's wrong now?" she inquired.

"I'm sorry, honey," he explained. "I'm a little embarrassed. I've got kneesels."

Harley then removed his shorts at which point Blanche exclaimed, "I see you've also got small cox."

* * *

Hollis and Irma got married and, that night, checked into a hotel. In order to balance out their lovemaking, Hollis gave the hotel clerk a big tip to fix their drinks. He had him put a dash of saltpeter in his wife's drink and a dash of Spanish Fly for his own.

But the bellboy got the drinks mixed up, and Hollis got the saltpeter, and Irma got the Spanish Fly. Next morning, Hollis came downstairs completely exhausted. The clerk said, "How did the drinks work out?"

"Well," said newlywed, "did you ever try to shove a pound of butter up a wildcat's ass with a wilted noodle?"

138

In Summer he said she was fair,
In Autumn her charms were still there,
    But he said to his wife
    In the Winter of life,
"There's no Spring in your old derriere."

*   *   *

The honeymoon is over when the husband asks for a night . . . off.

*   *   *

The bride refused to have intercourse with her new husband. Each time he tried on the wedding night she said, "Not yet. Wait till the spirit moves me."

Finally, after many hours of refusing, she turned to him suddenly and said, "Quick, honey, the spirit moves me."

"Well, let the spirit screw you. I've jacked off!"

*   *   *

Corbin complained of his wife's sexual appetite to a buddy at a bar. "We went to bed at nine," he explained, "and at eleven she said, 'How about it?' Then at twelve, 'Well, how about it?' At that point I got mad as hell and I said, 'How about what?' She said, 'How about getting off me so I can go take a piss.' "

Lori was about to marry Kip. She had been around but really loved Kip and was afraid he'd know she wasn't a virgin. So, she went to her gynecologist.

"Is there anything I can do to make my husband think he is the first man?"

"Well," said the M.D., "put a rubber band around your thigh. When you're near orgasm, just snap the rubber band. When he hears the snap, he'll think he just popped your cherry."

After the ceremony, the couple hurried to their honeymoon hotel. While Kip undressed, Lori stepped into a flimsy nightie, and also slipped a rubber band up around her thigh.

They jumped into bed and began making love. As Lori felt herself near orgasm she reached down, grabbed the rubber band and gave it a strong pluck.

"Hey," moaned Kip, "what was that?"

"Oh, honey," said Lori, "you must have popped my cherry."

"Really? Well, we had better pop it again because one of my balls is caught in it."

*   *   *

CHISELER

A man who goes stag
To a wife-swapping party

Kincaid crawled in bed with his wife and immediately started making overtures. "None of that stuff tonight," she mumbled. "I have to get up at 6 o'clock in the morning to start my washing!"

"That's okay," he replied. "If I'm not done by then, I'll just quit!"

*   *   *

Did you hear about the guy who handed his wife a vibrator and told her to buzz off?

*   *   *

Seated at a table in one of those intimate little French restaurants off Fifth Avenue, the young couple were studying the unfamiliar items on their menus.

"I never know what to ask for in these places," said the man.

"Ask for an ambulance," groaned the gal, "here comes my husband!"

*   *   *

There was a young German named Fritz
Who was subject to passionate fits,
    But his pleasure in life
    Was to suck off his wife
As he swung by his knees from her tits.

*   *   *

141

Oscar had been out on the town with a knockout blonde, and returned home just as the sun was rising.

As he was undressing, his wife stared at him. Finally, she asked through clenched teeth, ''Where's your underwear?''

He looked down and cried, ''My God! I've been robbed!''

Young Chester entered the living room of his home and sat down beside his mother. After a few minutes of deep thought he said, "Mom, is it true that people can be taken apart like machines?"

"Of course not," replied his mother. "Where did you hear such nonsense?"

"Well, just now, Daddy was talking to somebody on the phone," said the boy, "and I heard him say that last night he screwed the ass off his secretary."

* * *

HAPPILY MARRIED COUPLE

*A husband out with another
man's wife*

* * *

Matthew was extremely fat. His wife was quite petite. One night they attended a neighbor's barbecue. After several martinis, one of the guests took Matthew aside. "Say," he whispered, "how can a big guy like you manage to have intercourse with such a little woman?"

"Oh, I just sit back in an armchair and move her up and down on my lap," explained Matthew. "It's just like masturbating but you've got somebody to talk to!"

* * *

"My gracious, Mrs. Conlon," said her friend. "You must have had a terrible time finding names for your quadruplets, especially when you were expecting only twins."

"Oh, no, not at all," replied Mrs. Conlon. "I named two of them as I had planned and added two more. Now it's Adolph, Rudolph, Getoff and Stayoff."

*   *   *

A newly married couple living in the suburbs began a tradition of making love at 6:10 every day. He would get off work at 5:00, catch the train home, walk in the door at 6:05, and they would have sex at 6:10. Religiously.

After three months of wedded bliss, the bride caught pneumonia. The doctor placed her on Penicillin and after a week, only three pneumonia bugs survived.

The three Pneumococci, Will, Phil, and Bill, met in the vaginal cavity to try and figure out what to do, since it was obvious they were losing out to the Penicillin.

"Hey," said Will, "I'm gonna go down to the little toe, the Penicillin will never think of looking for me there!"

"I think I will go up near the hair," said Phil. "That's not one of our usual hangouts."

"Well, you guys do what you want," said Bill, "but as for me, when the old 6:10 pulls out, I'm gonna be on it!"

Talbot was sulking all the way to the hospital. Finally his wife, who was driving, groaned, "Look, if you don't want the vasectomy, say so and I'll go back on the Pill."

"It isn't that," he grumbled, "but did you have to tell the kids you were taking me to the doctor to get me fixed?"

* * *

Did you hear about the fellow who took his wife surfing but the tide kept bringing her back?

* * *

The Wall Street broker arrived home early one day to discover his wife in bed with a man.

Stunned and startled he blurted out, "What the hell is going on here?"

His wife smiled at him and replied, "Rodney, I forgot to tell you, I've gone public."

* * *

A mortician who practiced in Fife
Made love to the corpse of his wife
    "How could I know, Judge?
    She was cold, did not budge—
Just the same as she acted in life."

What's wrong with cocktail parties?
The men usually stand around getting stiff,
And the women are usually tight, but when
They get home, they frequently find
That neither is either.

*   *   *

Gately had just returned from a month-long trip to Chicago. Outside his office, he ran into his good pal Burke.

"Hey old buddy," said Burke, "what's wrong? Your eyes are so red and bloodshot!"

"It happened in Chicago," explained Gately. "First night there I met this very attractive woman in a cocktail lounge. We had a few drinks, one thing led to another, and she spent the night with me at my hotel. When I awoke the next morning, she was crying. She told me she was married and that she was ashamed of herself."

"Well, that got me to thinking about my wife and kids back here; so we both sat there on the edge of the bed and cried for about a half hour."

"But," said Burke, "that was four weeks ago. What's that got to do with your eyes being bloodshot today?"

"Listen," exclaimed Gately, "you can't sit and cry your eyes out every morning for four weeks without making them a little red!"

Mark came home early one afternoon and found his wife lying naked on the bed, breathing heavily. "Ruth, what's the matter?" he asked.

"I think I'm having a heart attack," she gasped.

Mark rushed downstairs to phone a doctor when his son came rushing in and screamed, "Daddy! Daddy! There's a naked man in the front closet!"

Mark opened the closet door and found his best friend cowering there. "For God's sake, Brian," screamed Mark, "Ruth is having a heart attack and here you are sneaking around scaring the children!"

A practical joker at the office told newly married Vic that all wives with brown eyes cheat. That afternoon, Vic rushed home, grabbed his wife by the shoulders, gazed into her eyes and hollered, "Aha, brown!"

Just then a guy stepped out of the closet and said, "How the hell did you know I was here?"

* * *

Adele heard that her ex-husband just arrived in town and decided to phone him. "Hello, Judd, darling. How are you? Why don't you come out and see me?"

"But, my dear," said her ex, "I'm a seriously married man now."

"Well, that didn't seem to bother you much when you were married to me."

* * *

Sitting in a St. Louis bar, a lonesome wife complained to the sexy bartender. "My husband is always away on business trips. I wonder what you would do *in my place*?"

* * *

An old couple, just groom and bride,
Were having a piece—when he died.
    The wife for a week
    Sat tight on his peak,
And bounced up and down as she cried.

Over a cocktail, a business exec confided to an associate, "My sex life has improved tremendously since my wife and I got twin beds."

"How can that be?" asked the coworker.

"Well," replied the exec, "hers is in Connecticut and mine's in New York."

*   *   *

Henderson sent a telegram home that he had been able to wind up his business trip early and would be home on Wednesday. When he walked into his condo, however, he found his wife, Trish, in bed with another man. Furious, he picked up his bag and stormed out. Out on the street, Henderson met his mother-in-law, told her what happened, and announced that he was filing for divorce in the morning.

"Give Trish a chance to explain before you do anything," begged the woman.

An hour later, his mother-in-law phoned Henderson at his club. "I knew Trish would have an explanation," said the woman. "She never received your telegram!"

*   *   *

The sudden entrance of a wife has caused many a secretary to change her position.

*　　*　　*

Lawyer: So you want to divorce him?

Blonde: Yes. I can't take any more. He's drunk night and day. He comes home at all hours of the morning, and never gives me any money.

Lawyer: What about sex?

Blonde: It was infrequent.

Lawyer: Is that one word or two?

*　　*　　*

A married woman and her lover were in the bedroom when she suddenly gasped, "Oh, my God. My husband's coming!"

"Where's your back door?" asked the lover.

"We don't have one," replied the wife.

"Where would you like one?"

*　　*　　*

One evening Wheeler's wife came home from a lingerie shop with a pair of $50 imported silk panties. She explained it by saying, "After all, dear, you wouldn't expect to find top quality perfume in a cheap bottle, would you?"

"No," snapped her husband, "and I wouldn't expect to find gift wrapping around a dead beaver, either!"

*　　*　　*

BENEATH THIS STONE
LIES MY WIFE MARIE,
COLD AND STIFF
AS SHE LAID UNDER ME.

Margaret came home with a package all wrapped up. "What's that?" asked her husband, Harold.

"It's a magic mirror," she answered, hanging it on the wall. "The salesman in the antique shop said it will grant any wish you make."

She then stood in front of the mirror and said, "Mirror, mirror on the wall—make my boobs the biggest of all!" And in a flash they began growing larger and larger until she had big beautiful breasts.

Then Harold stood in front of the mirror and said, "Mirror, mirror, show me more— let my pecker touch the floor."

And sure enough, his legs started getting shorter and shorter and . . .

Barlow turned out the bedroom light, turned to his wife and said, "Look, if you don't put some more action into it in the sack, I'm gonna go out and get me some strange stuff."

"Listen, Romeo," snapped the wife, "if you could somehow manage just a teensy inch more, you'd be into some strange stuff right here."

*　　*　　*

FRENCHMAN'S PHILOSOPHY

It's not nearly as important for a housewife to be able to make a good bed as it is for her to make a bed good.

*　　*　　*

Side by side they relaxed in bed, contentedly dragging on their cigarettes. Finally one of them broke the silence.

"You know," he said, "this wife-swapping wasn't such a bad idea. I only hope our wives are hitting it off this well!"

*　　*　　*

Meg and Rob were celebrating their tenth anniversary. "You can have anything you want for an anniversary present," announced Meg. "What would you like?"

"A blow job!" requested Rob.

That night in bed, Meg, doing it for the first time, made a great effort to please her mate. She got him thoroughly aroused and could tell he was getting close to a climax. "Honey," she asked, "what do I do when you come?"

"How do I know!" he replied, "I'm not a cocksucker!"

*   *   *

The surest sign of a man in love is when he divorces his wife.

*   *   *

Whitney and Ada were having breakfast. "Last night I dreamed they were auctioning off pricks," announced Ada. "Big ones went for $50 and the thick ones went for a $100."

"And how much did they get for the ones like mine?" asked the husband.

"Oh," said the wife, "those they were giving away for nothing!"

"I had a dream, too!" said Whitney. "I dreamed they were auctioning off cunts. The pretty ones went for $5,000 and the little, tight ones went for $10,000."

"And how much did they get for the ones like mine?"

"That's where they held the auction!"

*   *   *

A young bride was once heard to say,
"Oh dear, I am wearing away!
    The insides of my thighs
    Look just like mince pies,
For my husband won't shave every day."

Cockamania

The pharmacist walked up to a man loitering in the drugstore. "Please," he said, "don't smoke that cigar here!"

"But I just bought it here!" objected the man.

"Look," said the pharmacist, "we also sell laxatives!"

* * *

A LUCKY PERSON

Someone who stepped in shit and came up smelling like a rose

Berman returned home. He hadn't been in the house five minutes before he began to scream at his wife. "Who's your lover? Who came today to see you?"

"You're crazy!" answered his wife. "There was nobody here!"

"Don't try to fool me," shouted Berman. "I'm the only man in this house. Who was here today? The toilet seat is up!"

*　　*　　*

Finley had been hired to clean the lion's cage and he didn't like the job one little bit. He went to Trahern the keeper and asked, "What should I do if the lion rushes at me?"

"He won't," said Trahern.

"But suppose he does?"

"Throw something at him," said the keeper.

"But there's nothing in the cage to throw," insisted Finley.

"Listen," said the keeper, "if that lion rushes at you—there will be."

*　　*　　*

SIGN IN YELLOWSTONE NATIONAL PARK

Prevent Forest Fires
Pee on a Tree

What would you call a toilet-paper salesman on Fire Island?

Mary, Queen of Scotts.

* * *

The oldest son of the Shah of a Middle East country is called a Shan. One Shan was subject to epileptic seizures, and his father sent for a specialist to examine the boy.

The doctor said, "An examination wouldn't be sufficient. I want to be present during a seizure."

The Shah arranged for the physician to be near the Shan for twenty-four hours a day.

One evening the boy had a seizure, but the medical man was nowhere to be found. The Shah was enraged, and when the doctor was eventually located, the Shah screamed at him, "Where were you when the fit hit the Shan?"

* * *

There once was a lady named Muir
Whose mind was so frightfully pure
    That she fainted away
    At a friend's house one day
When she saw some canary manure.

* * *

There was a young girl from Wheeling
Who had a peculiar feeling.
　　She lay on her back
　　And opened her crack
And pissed all over the ceiling.

* * *

Bregar the play director was having great difficulty with the amateur actor he was rehearsing for a summer show.

"You've got to time it just right and say it with feeling," he said. "Let's take that line over again where you enter and say, 'Juliet, what have you done?' Stop after 'Juliet' and take a couple of short breaths and then put some umph into 'What have you done?' Get it?"

The aspiring actor nodded. They regrouped the players, and set the scene again. Then he re-entered:

"Juliet," he said, "Juliet (*sniff, sniff*). What have you done?"

* * *

Alice and Zach were strolling hand in hand through a wooded pasture outside Oklahoma City when she exclaimed, "Oh, a prairie pie!"

"Yeah," he agreed, "but which one of us stepped in it!"

* * *

Granville fancied himself as a liquor expert. One night at a Lake Tahoe bar he bet $100 that, blindfolded, he could taste any booze and identify the type and maker of it.

Pete, the barkeep, agreed and put the blindfold on Granville. The first drink was presented. Granville gulped half of it and said, "That's easy. It's rye . . . Canadian Club."

The bartender refilled the glass from another bottle, and Granville tasted. "Uh-huh," he said, "that's Scotch."

"But whose?" asked Pete.

"Ballantine's," was the reply.

"Right again," said Pete. "How about this one?"

Granville sipped and said, "Bourbon."

"Whose?"

"Old Granddad."

The crowd applauded.

Pete went into the men's room, returned shortly with a full glass, and gave it to Granville to taste. "Ooh!" he exclaimed. "That's urine."

"Right," said Pete. "But whose . . . ?"

* * *

"Isn't Hobart a classy fellow?"

"Sure is! He's the only guy I know who gets out of the shower to take a pee!"

* * *

Pettigrew was born with a golden screw in his navel. When he grew up, the golden screw became bothersome during love-making so Pettigrew decided to have it removed. He went to the Mayo Clinic, and was told that the golden screw could not be removed.

They sent him to a surgeon in Switzerland, who agreed that the screw could not be removed. The surgeon suggested a seer in Bombay.

Pettigrew went to India. The seer said that the screw could not and should not be removed. Pettigrew insisted, so the seer sent him to a holy man in Egypt.

The holy man said, "During the next full moon, go to the Great Sphinx, lie on your back naked, and repeat three times, 'Allah, please remove the golden screw from my navel.' "

The night of the full moon, Pettigrew went to the Great Sphinx, removed his clothing, lay on his back, and three times asked for Allah's help.

Suddenly there appeared a bright, shining dot. It came closer and closer. The object was a gold screwdriver. It hovered above him. Then slowly the screwdriver began to unscrew the golden screw. The screw was removed!

At last Pettigrew was rid of the golden screw! He leaped up and his ass fell off!!!

A beautiful Florida Miss
Simply thought it the apex of bliss,
    To jazz herself silly
    With the bud of a lily,
    Then go to the garden and piss.

*   *   *

Zeke, a small town nitwit, was about to visit Omaha. "Hey," said a friend, "don't you let them city slickers be puttin' anything over on you."

"Don't worry none about me," answered the yokel.

When Zeke arrived in the Windy City he passed a sign that said: *Billiards—Beer*. He walked inside and said to the bartender, "Gimme a glass of billiards."

"Ain't no such thing," said the barkeep.

"You got a sign out there that says you sell billiards, and I want a glass."

"I tell you there ain't no such drink."

"Listen, you can't put anything over on me. I got my rights. I want a glass of billiards."

The bartender grabbed a glass, turned his back to Zeke, and peed in it. The yokel took a big swig and said, "If I wasn't an experienced billiard drinker I'd swear that was piss!"

*   *   *

Why do women fart after they pee?

It's because women can't shake theirs, so they blow it dry.

* * *

Mrs. Van De Griff, a wealthy socialite, was giving a Long Island tea party when the water was turned off.

"Manuela," she told the maid, "make the tea from the water that's left in my bidet."

Mrs. Van De Griff then prepared the guests for any unusual flavor they might taste in it by telling them that the tea they were going to drink was imported specially for her from China, across Siberia, by camel train.

After tasting the tea, one elderly man grimaced.

"Don't you like it?" asked the hostess.

"Oh yes," he replied, "but I just got one of the camel's hairs caught in my teeth."

* * *

A cowboy born up in Butte
Found seven huge warts on his root.
  He put acid on these
  And now when he pees
He must finger the thing like a flute.

* * *

In 1912, during the great period of immigration, Danofsky left Pinsk and arrived in New York. He began wandering through the streets of Manhattan and, in a while, had to pee.

Danofsky spoke no English, and had no idea what an American did when he needed a restroom. His discomfort grew and finally he was in considerable pain. Danofsky walked into a building, made his way down the hall, and knocked on one of the doors.

The door opened about six inches and a hand came out, holding an empty bottle. The immigrant took it, and the door closed. He relieved himself in the bottle. Then he knocked again. The hand came out, put fifteen cents into the Russian's hand, and took the bottle. The door closed.

Danofsky resumed his walk more joyous than ever. Soon he had to go again. He knocked on another door, got the bottle, performed his function, and the hand gave him fifteen cents.

He quickly addressed a letter to his brother back in Pinsk. "Dear Boris," he wrote. "Come quick to America. In Pinsk, you are pissing away a fortune."

*   *   *

Then there's the new deodorant out called "Gone." You put it on and you disappear. Then all your friends stand around and say, "Where the hell is that smell coming from?"

*　　*　　*

Did you hear about the constipated accountant that couldn't budget, so he worked it out with a pencil?

*　　*　　*

PARTY POOPERS

*People who spike the punch
with prune juice*

*　　*　　*

Kuntz and Foster were standing outside a neighborhood saloon in Philadelphia late one winter night, and began emptying their bladders.

"It's an amazing thing," said Kuntz. "When I pee there seems to be nothing. When you pee it is like the rushing of a river, the beautiful sounds of a waterfall crashing on the rocks below. Why is that?"

"Because," said Foster, "I pee on the cobblestones. When you pee, it's on my overcoat."

169

In public wash rooms around the country there are now all kinds of modern conveniences. When Walton entered one he was not surprised to find the sign: *Your Wife away from Home*. Directly underneath it, was a hole.

He deposited the required amount, unzipped his pants, made the entry, and felt the most excruciating pain he had ever experienced.

Withdrawing, there tightly sewed on the end of it was a button.

*   *   *

Young Deward was driving his girl friend Inabelle home from a dance. They were on a country road when Deward felt the need to relieve himself. He stopped the car and said to Inabelle, "I gotta take a look at one of the rear tires."

He walked a few yards back of the car and then directed his aim into the roadside ditch. Immediately a volley of curses came from below.

Deward, standing on the roadway, called out, "Shhhhh for krysake! I've got a woman up here!"

And a voice in the darkness of the ditch shouted, "What the hell do you think I got down here—a sheep?"

*   *   *

Why do farts smell?
So deaf people can enjoy them, too.

*   *   *

Captain Cooper, the pilot of a DC 10, turned on the loudspeaker system and said, "We are landing at Los Angeles airport in two minutes . . . fasten your seat belts. . . . Hope you had a pleasant trip."

Then, forgetting to turn it off, he remarked to the co-pilot, "The first thing I'm gonna do when we land is take a dump, and the second thing I'm going to do is throw the harpoon into that blonde stewardess in the back cabin."

Embarrassed, the blonde hostess dashed to the cockpit to tell Cooper to shut up. She tripped in the aisle next to a little old lady who said, "Don't rush, dearie, he's got to do something else first!"

*   *   *

SIGN IN MEN'S ROOM

Please don't throw cigarette butts in the urinal. They clog the urinal, and they're difficult to light when they're soggy.

Fenton went to the doctor. After an examination the M.D. said, "You need an operation. I've got to remove your entire digestive system."

"What does that mean?" asked Fenton.

"For the rest of your life you will have to be fed rectally!"

"Rectally!" moaned Fenton.

After the operation the doc said, "You're going to be fine. Come to my office in a month."

Four weeks later Fenton was in the physician's examination room doing knee bends. The doctor watched him stand up and then squat and then stand. Finally, he said, "What are you doing?"

"I'm chewing tobacco!"

"All right!" said the doctor, "just don't spit!"

*   *   *

The difference between amnesia and magnesia is that the person with amnesia doesn't know where he is going.

*   *   *

"What do you think of Flushing, New York?"

"I think it's a great idea."

*   *   *

Have you heard about the new drink that has Vodka and Castor Oil?

It's called a Pile Driver

*   *   *

Tyler went to an out-of-the-way country hotel for a rest. On his first night, while walking around the grounds, he fell into a half-filled cesspool.

"Help!" he shouted. "Fire! Fire!"

Very soon the firemen, policemen, and all the other guests arrived and dragged him from the slimy, smelly pit.

"What's the idea of yelling, 'Fire'?" demanded the chief. "There's no fire here."

"What the hell did you want me to holler?" said Tyler. " 'Crap'?"

*   *   *

There was a show girl named Carter
Who was widely renowned as a farter.
　　Her deafening reports
　　At the Olympic sports
Made her much in demand as a starter.

*　　*　　*

Harper was sitting in an inside booth of an Oakland airport restroom. When he was through, Harper reached for toilet paper, and there was none. He looked down and saw two feet in the next booth so he said, "Excuse me over there, buddy, could you pass me some toilet paper? I don't have any."

"Sorry Mac, there's no toilet paper over here either."

"You have any newspaper?" asked Harper.

"No, I don't."

"Do you have a letter or an envelope or something?"

"Can't help you!"

"Well," asked Harper, "you got two fives for a ten?"

*　　*　　*

What's invisible and smells like carrots?
Rabbit farts.

*　　*　　*

When a girl can read the handwriting on the wall—she's in the wrong restroom.

*   *   *

Lloyd had a terrible problem. When other people passed gas with the usual "thhhurt," his was a loud "Honda." People would look around for the source of the smelly "Honda," while Lloyd tried to look innocent. He went from doctor to doctor, but no cause could be found despite extensive testing. In desperation, he wound up at an acupuncture clinic and explained to an old wrinkled Chinaman,

"I pass gas that sounds like 'Honda,' rather than 'thhhurt' like everyone else."

"Ah so," said the old one. "You have dental abcess. You need to go to a dentist."

"But you haven't even looked at me," said Lloyd.

"Trust me," said the elderly Chinese.

Lloyd went to his dentist, and sure enough, he had an abcessed tooth. The D.D.S. did a root canal and as Lloyd walked out the office door, he went "thhhurt!"

He rushed back to the old Chinaman and asked, "How could you possibly have known without examining me?"

"It is old Chinese saying: Abcess Makes the Fart Go Honda. . . ."

*   *   *

What's a foot stool?
A 12-inch shit.

*   *   *

Dalton telephoned his friend Walker at two o'clock in the morning. "I'm sorry to bother you."

"What do you want?" asked his friend.

"My hemorrhoids are killing me. I don't have any Preparation H. I can't see the proctologist 'til tomorrow. You had that trouble, what did you do?"

"You got any tea leaves in the house?"

"Yeah!"

"Boil them up, put them in your behind, it'll draw out the pain. . . . You'll be fine!"

Dalton tried it and he felt fine. Next morning he rushed to the doctor's office completely forgetting to remove the tea leaves. He got up on the examination table, bent over and said, "Well, doc, what do you see?"

"H'm" said the M.D. "I see an ocean voyage. . . ."

*   *   *

MANURE

*What a farmer puts on
his strawberries*

*   *   *

Gary earned only $60 a week, yet he began wooing a wealthy Brentwood girl. Her father was angry. "You could never keep my daughter in the manner she is accustomed to. Your $60 a week couldn't keep her in toilet paper!"

"I'm grateful for you being so frank," said Gary. "I don't think I want to marry your daughter anyhow, if she's that full of shit."

*   *   *

Idella was awaiting the arrival of her boyfriend Bobby Joe, and while sitting in the living room she let out an enormous fart. To eliminate the odor she quickly grabbed a can of air freshener and sprayed it all over the room.

When Bobby Joe arrived he sniffed a few times and said, "I hate to say anything but it smells like somebody just shit in a pine tree."

*   *   *

Some practical jokers decided to play a sad joke on Kane, the village idiot. One of the jokesters had a pet monkey, to whom he gave a cork and instructions. That night, while Kane was asleep, the monkey climbed through his window and inserted the cork into his anus.

Unaware of the presence of the cork, Kane did not have a bowel movement for several weeks, and his torso began to swell. When he told the jokers of his discomfort and swelling, they suggested that he might be pregnant. Much to their surprise, Kane was delighted and went around telling people of the forthcoming blessed event.

The jokers realized that the joke had gone too far, and that night, while the dimwit was asleep, the monkey again entered the bedroom through the window. He took a firm grip on the cork and pulled it out. The released excrement and gas caused a loud blast; the room was splattered, and the monkey, dazed.

The blast woke up Kane who saw the monkey, cradled it in his arms, and said, "You're a hairy little fellow, and you're full of shit, but you're mine, all mine."

*　　*　　*

A Virginia farmer named Hyde
Fell down in an outhouse and died.
　　His unfortunate brother
　　Then fell down another
And now they're in graves side-by-side

*　　*　　*

On summer vacation, Burl came home to the farm from college and saw his father shoveling all the manure from the outhouse onto the strawberry patch.

"Pop, there's an easier way to do that," said the farmer's son.

They went to the store, got some dynamite and rigged it up under the outhouse so it would blow the excrement all over the strawberries. They didn't know grandma was using the outhouse, so when they set off the explosion, it blew grandma right through the air into the strawberries.

"Are you all right, grandma?" asked the farmer.

"I'm fine," said the old lady. "But I sure am glad I didn't let that one go in the kitchen."

WILDE ON WILDE

I love humor. I've spent over 30 years studying, analyzing, researching, teaching, performing and writing it. The fascination started in Jersey City where I was born in 1928. As a kid during the Depression we had to scratch hard to make a buck and making jokes was a way of life.

After a two-year stint in the Marine Corps, where I found I could make leathernecks laugh, I worked my way through the University of Miami, Florida, doing a comedy act at the hotels. After graduating, I entertained in night clubs and theaters all over the U.S. I got to play Vegas and Tahoe and the other big time spots being the ''supporting'' comedian for Ann-Margret, Debbie Reynolds, Pat Boone, and a lot of others.

I've done acting roles on *Mary Tyler Moore, Rhoda, Sanford & Son* and other sitcoms; performed on Carson, Griffin, Douglas and did a bunch of TV commercials.

This is my 30th joke book. I'm also proud of the two serious works I've done on comedy technique: THE GREAT COMEDIANS TALK ABOUT COMEDY and HOW THE GREAT COMEDY

WRITERS CREATE LAUGHTER. Both books have been called "definitive" works on the subject.

My books have sold over 7,000,000 copies which makes them the largest selling humor series in publishing history. And while I'm blowing my own horn here, the best thing I ever did was to marry Maryruth Poulos, a really talented writer from Wyoming.

SPECIAL MONEY SAVING OFFER

Now you can have an up-to-date listing of Bantam's hundreds of titles plus take advantage of our unique and exciting bonus book offer. A special offer which gives you the opportunity to purchase a Bantam book for only 50¢. Here's how!

By ordering any five books at the regular price per order, you can also choose any other single book listed (up to a $4.95 value) for just 50¢. Some restrictions do apply, but for further details why not send for Bantam's listing of titles today!

Just send us your name and address plus 50¢ to defray the postage and handling costs.

BANTAM BOOKS, INC.
Dept. FC, 414 East Golf Road, Des Plaines, Ill 60016

Mr./Mrs./Miss/Ms. _____
(please print)

Address _____

City_____ State_____ Zip_____

FC—3/84